# CHICANO MOVEMENT
## F O R   B E G I N N E R S ®

# CHICANO MOVEMENT
## FOR BEGINNERS®

**WRITTEN AND ILLUSTRATED BY MACEO MONTOYA**

Foreword by Ilan Stavans

**FOR BEGINNERS®**

For Beginners LLC
155 Main Street, Suite 211
Danbury, CT 06810 USA
www.forbeginnersbooks.com

A For Beginners® Documentary Comic Book

Cataloging-in-Publication information is
available from the Library of Congress.

ISBN-13 # 978-1-939994-64-6 Trade

Manufactured in the United States of America

For Beginners® and Beginners Documentary Comic
Books® are published by For Beginners LLC.

First Edition

10 9 8 7 6 5 4 3 2 1

FOR ANGIE CHABRAM,
WHO KEEPS THROWING PUNCHES.

# CONTENTS

# FOREWORD
## BY ILAN STAVANS

Democracy is rowdy and boisterous and insatiable. Its strength lies in the fact that it is always unfinished, a work in progress in which history is always being reassessed by constant social change. This means that ideas and emblems and figures go in and out of fashion.

Take the term *Chicano*. Once a moniker symbolizing empowerment, it seems to have undergone an eclipse. Mexican Americans use it only sparingly today, often to refer to the Chicano Movement, also known as *El Movimiento*, the upheaval that sought to reconfigure, during the Civil Rights era, their place in the tapestry that is the United States. It seldom shows up to describe the present.

To some degree, this is because as a minority, Mexican Americans have become part of a larger identity rubric, "Latinos," encompassing them as well as millions of others with origins in Latin America and the Caribbean (Salvadorans, Dominicans, Colombians, Cubans, Puerto Ricans, et al). But there are other reasons: unlike Black Liberation, the Chicano Movement, in truth, was less about race than about class. And a few of its leaders, César Chávez among them, made what in hindsight appear to be tactical mistakes. A few were against immigration, for instance, which is the equivalent of being against their own origins. And their connection with Mexico, where many of them traced their roots, was faulty, disengaged, and even negligent.

It pains me deeply that the Civil Rights era continues to be seen, by most people, in black and white, not in full color. That is, the plight of other ethnic groups, including Mexican Americans, Puerto Ricans, and Filipinos, whose struggle for self-determination is equally important, is seldom considered integral to it. In the last few decades, streets, schools, and community centers in the Southwest have been named after Chávez and other Chicano historical figures. Yet their achievements have gone largely undigested by the nation as a whole. Chávez himself said that in his fight he drew strength from despair but, unfortunately, that despair is seldom acknowledged in any meaningful way in the public sphere. He believed that "history will judge societies and their institutions ... by how effective they respond to the needs of the poor and the helpless." Well, on that front as well, the United States leaves much to be desired.

Maceo Montoya is intent on reawakening us. He is the son of a leading Chicano activist and artist, Malaquias Montoya, and a sibling of poet Andrés Montoya, author of the award-winning *The Iceworker Sings,* who died tragically, of leukemia, at the age of 31. A painter as well as scholar, he has produced a spirited "For Beginners" book that pays tribute to the legacy of Mexican illustrator Eduardo del Río, aka *Rius,* by looking at *El Movimiento* with fresh eyes. It mixes highbrow and pop culture in engaging, thought-provoking ways. At its core, it is, in my view, a family affair, an attempt by Professor Montoya to reconsider the past his forebears shaped, a past that lives inside him and the rest of us, and whose place in the future is still up for grabs.

The Chicano Movement might look dead, Montoya suggests, but its spins continue to define us, whether we acknowledge it or not. It is time to fashion its ideals back to the present.

*Mexican-born educator, author, and cultural critic Ilan Stavans is Lewis-Sebring Professor in Latin American and Latino Culture at Amherst College. He is the author of numerous book-length works, including* Latino U.S.A.: A Cartoon History; *the editor of numerous others, including* The Norton Anthology of Latino Literature; *a prolific contributor to scholarly journals and anthologies; and a popular television and radio commentator.*

# PROLOGUE

I grew up in a Chicano home, which is to say, my family considered the Chicano Movement to be very much alive, and its important events and leaders were mentioned with great frequency and seemingly at every opportunity. As a child in the 1980s and early '90s, I was exposed (often dragged) to countless political rallies and cultural events, and everyone else at these functions seemed to share the same base of knowledge about the Chicano Movement, not only why it was important and who was involved, but also why its goal to create a more just and equitable society continued to be relevant. So I have to admit that when I finally ventured off into the wider world, it was somewhat of a surprise to learn that whenever I mentioned the Chicano Movement, or even the word Chicano, most people didn't know what I was talking about.

As the heyday of the Chicano Movement, roughly 1965–1975, fades further into history, and as more and more of its important figures pass on, so too does knowledge of its significance. Thus, this book is a small attempt to stave off historical amnesia. It seeks to shed light on the multifaceted civil rights struggle that formed the Chicano Movement. Just as African Americans in the 1960s fought to end centuries of racism, discrimination, and injustice, so did Mexican Americans. From California to Texas and well into the Midwest and even the East Coast, young and old emerged from the shadows to demand their rightful place in American society. The Chicano Movement, also known as *El Movimiento,* galvanized the Mexican American community, from laborers to student activists, giving them not only a political voice to combat prejudice and inequality, but also a new sense of cultural awareness and ethnic pride.

Beyond commemorating the past, this book seeks to reaffirm the goals and spirit of the Chicano Movement for the simple reason that many of the critical issues Mexican American activists first brought to the nation's attention in the late 1960s and early '70s—educational disadvantage, endemic poverty, political exclusion, and social bias—remain as pervasive as ever almost a half-century later. As the Latino population in the United States continues to grow, not just in the Southwest but across the country, these issues will assume greater prominence in the national discourse. As this occurs, all Americans will be wise to take note of the spirit and legacy of the Chicano Movement, charting a way forward with a deeper understanding of its successes, its failures, its lessons, and its inspirations.

—Maceo Montoya

# 1

## BACKGROUND TO A MOVEMENT

# WHAT'S A CHICANO? DEPENDS.

NO ONE EVER OWNED EXISTENTIALISM. IT HAS
ALWAYS MEANT DIFFERENT THINGS TO DIFFERENT
PEOPLE. IT WAS NEVER A SINGLE DOCTRINE THAT
WAS LAID DOWN DEFINITIVELY BY ONE PERSON
OR GROUP. EACH PIECE OF WRITING ABOUT IT IS
DIFFERENT, EACH BEARS AN INDIVIDUAL STAMP.
THERE WAS NO SINGLE VOICE OF AUTHORITY, SO ITS
DEFINITION HAS ALWAYS HAD BLURRY EDGES. . . .
IT COULD BE SEEN AS A HISTORICAL NECESSITY OR
INEVITABILITY, AN EFFORT TO ADAPT TO A NEW
CONFLUENCE OF CULTURAL AND HISTORICAL FORCES.

DAVID COGSWELL, *EXISTENTIALISM FOR BEGINNERS*

Odd as this may seem, if you remove "existentialism" from the above quote and replace it with "Chicano" you get a pretty good understanding of the term and its complicated place in Mexican American history. Armando Rendón, in his landmark 1970 book, *Chicano Manifesto*, wrote, "I am Chicano. What it means to me may be different than what it means to you." More than two decades later, the Chicano poet and novelist Benjamin Alire Sáenz wrote, "There is no such thing as the Chicano voice: there are only Chicano and Chicana *voices*." To this day, the term "Chicano" maintains its blurry edges, but it continues to reflect a meaningful way of thinking about the confluence of cultural and historical forces—in short, about life.

Many activists in the Chicano Movement pointed to an etymology of the word "Chicano" rooted in the clash between Spain and Mesoamerica, specifically the Spanish conquest of the Valle de Mexica and its people, the Mexicas (more commonly known as the Aztecs), in the 16th century. Mexica was pronounced *Meshica*,

THE CHICANO DILEMMA
TO BE OR NOT
TO BE!

but lacking a letter equivalent, the Spaniards changed the "sh" to an "x"—hence Mexica, or México, or Mexicanos. *Shicano* was simply short for Me*shicanos*. For these early activists, then, the term Chicano served two purposes: it made a connection not only to their Mexican roots, but also to their indigenous past. Compare that to the term "Hispanic," which many Chicanos rejected because it references only the connection to Spain, basically negating half an identity and history.

Historically, however, most Mexican Americans knew the word Chicano through its common usage, mainly as a derogatory label for Mexicans who had become "gringofied," linguistically and culturally, when they immigrated to the United States. *Pocho*, literally meaning rotten fruit, was another common label. These terms indicated a people stuck in between, who were neither American nor Mexican, who could speak neither proper English nor proper Spanish, who had forgotten their Mexican culture as they adopted the values and attitudes of North American society—in essence, a lost people. Never to be truly American, lapsed as Mexicans, they were a people without a country.

But Mexican Americans also used the term Chicano to describe themselves, and usually in a lighthearted way, or as a term of endearment, maybe even as self-effacement. Doing so expressed awareness that they had not just departed from or forgotten their Mexican origins, but that they had actually become a unique community. When Mexican Americans began identifying as Chicanos, it was a form of self-affirmation; it reflected the consciousness that their experience living in between nations, histories, cultures, and languages was uniquely and wholly theirs. This is what gave birth to a sense of community, a people: los Chicanos.

Lastly, and maybe most importantly, civil rights activists who called themselves Chicanos emphasized the fact that it was a name not given to them or placed on them by an outsider, but a name that they had chosen themselves. That choice reflected the Movimiento's greater goal of self-determination, standing up against and rejecting the Mexican American community's long-suffering history of racism, discrimination, disenfranchisement, and economic exploitation in the United States (more on that soon).

# DINNER PARTY FOR EL MOVIMIENTO

Let's say this is not a book but a dinner party where you invite all the key figures from the Chicano Movement to discuss their role in this tumultuous period. Unfortunately, the evening would already be off to a bad start. Why? Well, you couldn't possibly invite everyone, but you'd be expected to. One of the main currents of the Movimiento was to bring attention to *all* the struggles of the Mexican American community—whether those of a soldier in the Vietnam War, a field-worker in California, or a university student—and seeing them as one. And what is a dinner party if not an affair that includes a chosen few and excludes others?

But we get past that. Your dinner party must proceed, space is limited, and a guest list is in order. You definitely want to invite César Chávez, a national hero on par with other inspirational leaders whose faces have graced the cover of *Time* magazine, stamps, and countless posters in grade-school classrooms. Dinner with César alone would be intimidating, so you attempt to balance his saintly demeanor with that of his sister in nonviolence, the rabble-rouser Dolores Huerta.

The duo is first to arrive, and your dinner party and history lesson are solidly underway. Dolores leads the conversation, and soon you have a thorough understanding of the United Farm Workers (UFW) and their struggle against powerful and exploitative California growers. But you're surprised to learn that César never considered himself a Chicano leader; nor did most of his fellow farmworkers consider themselves Chicanos. But before you can ask him to explain, in walks a man who effusively announces that he is the cricket in the lion's ear, none other than Reies López Tijerina from New Mexico.

In the manner of a soapbox preacher, Reies launches into a long discourse on his efforts to reclaim the lands stripped away from the Indo-Hispano people of New Mexico following the

Mexican-American War and the 1848 Treaty of Guadalupe Hidalgo (which granted the United States about half of Mexico's territory). Reies recounts in vivid detail his persecution at the hands of New Mexican authorities, but after a half-hour and no signs of stopping, you begin to worry that no one else will be able to get a word in edgewise. Reies is in the middle of his story about the ill-fated Tierra Amarilla courthouse raid of 1967 when he is interrupted by the arrival of Rodolfo "Corky" Gonzalez, who, by way of introduction, begins reciting his epic poem of Chicano identity, *I am Joaquín*.

When Corky finishes his fiery recitation, he announces, much

to your consternation, that participants of the Chicano National Youth and Liberation Conference have followed him all the way from Denver, Colorado. As if on cue, in walks a group of boisterous young people, many of them with long hair and wearing ponchos and overalls. They quiet down only when you answer their calls for pens and paper so they can work on updating the goals of their so-called "spiritual plan."

Just as you're about to make your way back to the dinner table, a young man introducing himself as José Angel Gutiérrez walks through the door accompanied by yet another large group, this one hailing from Crystal City, Texas. Carrying lawn signs and campaign buttons, they identify themselves as members of La Raza Unida Party.

When you explain that there are not enough seats at the table, they make their way to the living room, where they find a telephone (the old rotary kind) and take turns calling potential voters.

With all the hubbub, you almost miss the arrival of a quiet, distinguished-looking man, a little older than most in attendance, who appears out of place. He introduces himself as the *Los Angeles Times* journalist Ruben Salazar. But before you can show him to the table, the front door opens and in walks a cadre of stern-faced young men and women, all dressed in khaki and brown. They stand at attention like soldiers in formation and bark out that they are the Brown Berets, defenders of the Chicano barrio.

The house is ready to burst, and you cringe as more commotion outside draws you to the window. You hear chants.

"What's going on?" you ask, afraid to open the door.

A participant of the youth conference informs you that the Chicana Caucus has organized a protest against your dinner party on account of the fact that so few women were invited. Soon the protesters make their way inside, and between their chants decrying patriarchy and demanding that their voices be heard, Corky reciting his poem again (upon request), the youth reading one platform after another, the pollsters making phone calls, and the general din of one explanation after another of this and that event, you can hardly hear yourself think. At wit's end, you cry out that what you wanted was a quiet little dinner party for the leaders and luminaries of the Chicano Movement to fill you in on the important events and ideas, that invitations had been sent out, and that the invitations did not say "plus one" or "plus two" and certainly not "plus fifty" and that you'd appreciate if everyone left at once.

Suddenly there is silence. Someone, you don't know who, says that if quiet is what you wanted then you've missed the point of a movement. You are unswayed. Guests, both invited and uninvited, begin to file out. You avoid César Chávez's eyes. When everyone has departed, you begin putting the house back together. Just as you're finally catching your breath, you're startled to hear the front door swing open.

In stomps a giant man with bulging, manic eyes, immediately demanding to know where the liquor cabinet is located. He introduces himself as the Brown Buffalo. He assumes you've heard of him, and when you tell him you haven't, he declares that he's the most radical of radical Chicano lawyers, Oscar Zeta Acosta. He locates

GLORIA ANZALDUA AND OSCAR ZETA ACOSTA

the liquor, pours himself a glass, and sits at the table. "Wasn't there supposed to be dinner?" he asks.

After loading his plate full of food, the Brown Buffalo, as he insists on being called, offers his version of the Chicano Movement, starting with his childhood. As he recounts his hang-ups about race and his forever frustrated quest to fit the American ideal or achieve the American dream, it dawns on you that Oscar's version of the Chicano Movement never deviates from his own point of view as the central protagonist. He grows angry, he sheds tears, he reveals details that make you uncomfortable, and just when you think he'll never stop, he passes out after one too many drinks.

As you clear the table, you hope you've seen the last of it all. But soon you hear a gentle knock at the door. With trepidation you open it, half expecting to find an even larger Brown Buffalo. Instead, you find a small woman with short hair and a kind smile. "I'm sorry I'm late," she says. "My name is Gloria Anzaldúa." You invite the Chicana scholar inside and she looks around, taking stock of the place. "Where is everybody?"

You give her the rundown of the night's events, culminating with the Brown Buffalo asleep in the dining room.

Anzaldúa smiles and says, "All that you describe sounds about right. It's all part of us. The Movimiento was a big dream with big personalities, and with that came big disappointments. But we shared one thing in common."

"What was that?" you ask.

"A desire to be heard. To no longer be erased."

You wait expectantly for Gloria to tell her version of the Chicano Movement, but instead she goes to the dining room table and finds Oscar snoring loudly. She starts to rustle him awake.

"Isn't he better off asleep?" you caution.

Gloria shakes her head. "I don't want to make this journey alone. We were all in it together…"

The dinner party is basically over, so let's return to the book at hand. It is fitting, though, that the last two guests presented such a study in contrasts. Always a fringe figure, Oscar Zeta Acosta—a lawyer, novelist, and drug enthusiast who disappeared mysteriously in Mazatlán, Mexico, in 1974, never to be heard from again—perhaps represents an amalgamation of the radical, at times militantly overzealous aspects of the movement, which in many ways extinguished itself by the mid-1970s. Gloria Anzaldúa came along a few years later, and her Chicana feminist writings—a combination of the scholarly, the polemical, the personal, and the poetic—represent a re-centering of the Chicano Movement and its ideals. With the political upheaval of the late 1960s and early '70s already fading into memory, Anzaldúa's seminal work, *La Frontera/Borderlands*, published in 1987, called on not just Chicanas and Chicanos, but everyone, to live up to the Movimiento's ideal of liberating all people discriminated against and shunted aside by dominant society, whether for reasons of class, race, gender, or sexual preference.

# 500 YEARS OF CONQUEST, COLONIZATION, DISENFRANCHISEMENT, AND EXPLOITATION IN A NUTSHELL

Just as the African American struggle for civil rights pointed to the harmful legacy of three centuries of slavery in the United States, Chicanos also pointed to historical roots of their modern-day conditions. In the 1960s, as Chicanos fought against extreme poverty, working conditions in the fields, the racism and discrimination they experienced in schools and society at large, and their lack of political representation, they started to understand that what they were experiencing didn't just happen all of a sudden, or in isolation. Rather, they came to recognize that it was part of a larger history of colonization, exploitation, and displacement, first by Spain, then by a succession of Mexican dictatorships, and finally by the United States. In effect, Chicanos sought to reconcile and rectify a pattern of suffering that tied back to the Spanish conquest of the Americas.

From that long history, activists in the Chicano Movement would return time and again to the following historical injustices and conflicts: the Spanish conquest of the Americas; Manifest Destiny and the betrayal of the Treaty of Guadalupe Hidalgo; Pancho Villa, Emiliano Zapata, and the fight for land and liberty in the Mexican Revolution; and, lastly, border conflict, second-class citizenship, and mass deportation.

## THE CONQUEST

Chicano activists became aware of their indigenous roots and took pride in the fact that they were descendants of an advanced civilization, but they also understood that they were mestizos: half Indian and half Spanish, a mixed race born of brutal conquest. The Spanish conquistador Hernán Cortés and his band of soldiers conquered the great Aztec Empire in only two years. They were aided by the superstitious Aztec belief that Cortés and his men were gods, maybe even Quetzalcoatl, the feathered serpent god who was pale-skinned, had a beard, and was predicted to return to Mexico in what was the European calendar year of 1519 (the very year of Cortés's arrival). In fact, the Aztec emperor Montezuma II sent emissaries to greet the newly arrived Spaniards with gifts of gold, hoping they would be satiated.

# LA MALINCHE

SERIOUSLY? YOU'RE BLAMING ME FOR EVERYTHING?

Cortés succeeded because he was able to forge alliances with the many tribes that the Aztecs had previously subjugated. He did so with the help of La Malinche, an enslaved Indian girl who served as an interpreter and guide and helped Cortés negotiate the warring tribes. She also bore Cortés a son, a mestizo, and his progeny: the new *mestizaje*, or mixed race. In the process, La Malinche became a complex symbol to Mexicans: not only was she the mistress of Cortés, the brutal conqueror, but she was also a mother complicit in her own people's destruction. Later, Chicana feminists would counter the notion that La Malinche had "sold out" her people. Instead, they saw that she had *survived* and thrived despite her trying circumstances and limited options, a spirit to be emulated rather than scorned.

Seeking this very fortune, the conquistadores were only spurred on further. Although Cortés and his men were greatly outnumbered, they had other advantages, especially superior weaponry and diseases for which the Indians had no immunity. Not long after Cortés landed, a smallpox epidemic broke out that decimated the indigenous population. Having conquered the great Mesoamerican cities and broken the spirits of the native people, Spain was able to impose its language, institutions, and most importantly, its religion, Catholicism, on its new subjects. They also exploited the natives for their labor, especially in mining and agriculture. In the three centuries following the conquest, New Spain enriched itself on the backs of Indians.

# BARTOLOMÉ DE LAS CASAS,

a Spaniard and Dominican friar, was the first ordained priest in the Americas. Over time he became highly critical of his countrymen's brutality toward the indigenous population. The following excerpt is from his *A Short Account of the Destruction of the Indies* (1542):

*The common ways mainly employed by the Spaniards who call themselves Christian and who have gone there to extirpate those pitiful nations and wipe them off the earth is by unjustly waging cruel and bloody wars. Then, when they have slain all those who fought for their lives or to escape the tortures they would have to endure,*

*that is to say, when they have slain all the native rulers and young men (since the Spaniards usually spare only the women and children, who are subjected to the hardest and bitterest servitude ever suffered by man or beast), they enslave any survivors. With these infernal methods of tyranny they debase and weaken countless numbers of those pitiful Indian nations. Their reason for killing and destroying such an infinite number of souls is that the Christians have an ultimate aim, which is to acquire gold, and to swell themselves with riches in a very brief time. . . .*

## Your Land is My Land, from California to the...

The Mexican-American War (1846–1848) is widely seen as a war of aggression instigated by the United States with the sole purpose of acquiring more territory, which they did: over half of Mexico. As a result, Chicano activists more than a century later emphasized their bitterness at being treated as foreigners on land that was once theirs. Manifest Destiny was the commonly held belief among 19th-century American citizens that it was their God-given right to own all the territory from the Atlantic Ocean to the Pacific Ocean and beyond. Never mind that Native Americans and the citizens of other countries already called it home. If the land could be conquered, then it belonged to the conqueror. Inherent in this belief, of course, was a notion of racial and cultural superiority. When Tennessean James K. Polk, an ardent proponent of Manifest Destiny, was elected president of the United States in 1844, he ran on a platform advocating the annexation of Texas, technically still part of Mexico even though

Texas had seceded from Mexico in 1836. Once Texas was annexed in 1845, President Polk set his sights westward, purportedly sending troops to "protect" Texas against attack but in reality seeking to acquire all the territory west of Texas. Both countries mobilized for war, and tensions bubbled over into outright conflict in 1846.

In the two years of fighting, the United States handily defeated Mexico, which had been weakened by debt and political turmoil. Its complete surrender resulted in the Treaty of Guadalupe Hidalgo in 1848. Mexico recognized the secession of Texas and lost what is now California, Nevada, Utah, New Mexico, Arizona, and parts of Colorado, Kansas, and Wyoming. Thousands of Mexicans living in these territories became U.S. citizens. The treaty explicitly guaranteed them rights to their land, language, religion, customs, and civil rights, but very quickly this proved not to be the case. Anglo-American settlers occupied their territory, Spanish and Mexican land grants were ignored or dismissed by the courts, and the new Mexican Americans were treated as a conquered people and second-class citizens.

# JUAN CORTINA

A large Texas landowner, Juan Cortina became a hero to Mexican Americans when, in 1859, he witnessed Brownsville marshall and former Texas Ranger Bob Spears brutally pistol-whip an old vaquero who once worked on Cortina's ranch. Cortina responded by shooting Spears, rescuing the old vaquero, and then crossing the border into Mexico. Two months later, he returned to Texas leading a group of 70 men, proclaiming that they would avenge the wrongs committed against Tejanos (Texas Mexicans) by

Anglo-Texans and that they would fight for the rights guaranteed by the Treaty of Guadalupe Hidalgo. The border war lasted ten tumultuous years, resulting in violence, destruction, and increased animosity between Tejanos and Anglo-Texans. Referred to as the "Robin Hood of the Rio Grande," Cortina became an enduring symbol of resistance against Anglo domination.

## THE MEXICAN REVOLUTION AND ITS HEROES

Whether ruled by Spanish colonial authority or Mexican strongmen, the Mexican masses worked to make other men rich. In the early 20th century, however, the Mexican Revolution and its heroes showed them that it was possible to fight against injustice. As a Spanish colony, Mexico and its people were exploited for the profit of the mother country and its representatives. When Mexico won its independence from Spain in 1821, the country continued to be operated for the benefit of the upper classes while the great majority of Mexicans lived in poverty. After too many coups and civil wars to count, Porfirio Díaz came to power in 1876 and ruled Mexico with an iron fist for the next 35 years. He brought stability to Mexico, but he did so with dictatorial control, using fear and oppression. He strengthened the economy, but he also sold off Mexico's resources to foreign powers, including the United States, enriching himself and his associates. Land was especially concentrated in the hands of the very few.

Liberal opposition to the *Porfiriato*, as Díaz's reign was called, grew in the early years of 20th century. Francisco Madero, a prominent liberal and champion of democracy, challenged Díaz for the presidency and was arrested, which spurred government opponents to call for Díaz's resignation. Quickly losing control, Díaz resigned in May 1911, paving the way for Madero to be elected president that fall.

But change didn't happen fast enough, and other revolutionaries rose to the fore—in particular two heroes of the Mexican Revolution (and later, the Chicano Movement): Pancho Villa and Emiliano Zapata. Villa in the north of Mexico and Zapata in the south fought on behalf of the Mexican poor, demanding that the revolution not simply replace the old aristocrats with new ones, but that it serve the impoverished, landless, and illiterate common man. Zapata's slogan *Tierra y Libertad* ("Land and Liberty") became a rallying cry for the peasant masses. Villa's brave exploits, including raiding an American town in New Mexico, made him a symbol of resistance against both the Mexican aristocracy and U.S. imperialism.

EMILIANO ZAPATA

PANCHO VILLA

LA ADELITA

The Mexican Revolution lasted an entire decade (1910–1920) and created massive upheaval and displacement. Tens of thousands of Mexicans fled the violence for the safety of the north, many of them poor, desperate, and hungry for work in the fledgling industries of the southwestern United States. This wave of immigration changed the landscape considerably. Seventy-five years after California became part of the United States, Los Angeles had the largest population of Mexicans outside of Mexico City.

## "LA ADELITA"

is a famous corrido, or ballad, from the Mexican Revolution. Although it was based on a real female soldier, the term *La Adelita* became synonymous with a woman warrior or *soldadera*. Later Chicana activists identified with La Adelita not simply as women accompanying the troops to perform domestic duties, but fighting for change as soldiers themselves.

## SECOND-CLASS CITIZENSHIP

For the hundred years following the Mexican-American War, Mexican Americans faced much of the same systematic discrimination and racism directed toward blacks in the Jim Crow South, including routine violence and intimidation, and countless lynchings. The law, whether represented by the courts, vigilante justice, or the hated Texas Rangers, was notoriously harsh on Mexican Americans. Many Mexican Americans were pushed off their lands, and those that fought back were treated like outlaws. Joaquín Murrieta, Tiburcio Vásquez, and Gregorio Cortez are just a few of the so-called bandits or outlaws that the Mexican American community saw as heroes for standing up to Anglo-American authority.

As Mexican immigration to the United States increased (and not just to California and Texas, but also to cities like Chicago) so did xenophobia and anti-immigrant backlash. Popular portrayals, agitated by the media during the Mexican Revolution and World War I, presented Mexicans as perpetrators of violence, sedition, and vice. Ultimately, they were seen as useful only for their cheap labor; industries such as the railroad, meat packing in the Midwest, steal and coal mining, and especially agriculture, depended on them.

Beyond that, in the society at large, Mexican Americans were pushed to the margins. Spanish was prohibited in schools and public institutions, laws were enforced that segregated Mexican Americans from whites, and in all but a few pockets of the Southwest, Mexican Americans were excluded almost entirely from the political process. During the Great Depression of the 1930s, anti-immigrant hysteria resulted in the mass repatriation of several hundred thousand Mexican nationals and their children, many of whom were born in the United States. Again in the 1950s, Operation Wetback resulted in the deportation of thousands of Mexican workers.

Because Chicano activists saw themselves as defenders of a long abused and subjugated community, they identified strongly with aspects of their history that fit that narrative—as enslaved Indians,

THESE FRUITS AND VEGETABLES ARE SIMPLY DELICIOUS.

indebted Mexican peons, or Mexican American farmers at the mercy of U.S. authorities. For this reason, despite being descended from both Spanish conquerors and conquered Indians, Chicanos identified more with their Indian side. The Mexican people had been exploited for their labor, their culture had been stripped away, and Chicanos felt that American society continued to perpetrate the same wrongs on them. And even though most Chicanos in the 1960s were descended from Mexicans who had immigrated to the United States *after* the Mexican-American War, they still saw the Southwest as land that was stolen from them, as well as further evidence of U.S. imperialist aggression. Lastly, as they suffered the indignities of second-class citizenship in the United States, Chicanos didn't need to look any farther than the Mexican Revolution for examples of the poor and disenfranchised rising up to fight injustice. A quote attributed to Emiliano Zapata was frequently cited to encourage Chicanos to stand up for their rights: "It is better to die on your feet than to live on your knees."

## PRECURSORS TO THE MOVEMENT

The generation that preceded the Chicano Movement was known as the "Mexican-American Generation" and was typified by its hope of assimilating, just as other ethnic European immigrants had before them, into the melting pot of American society. These Mexican Americans of the 1940s and 1950s were farther removed from Mexico than their immigrant parents or grandparents and believed that by adopting mainstream American cultural attitudes and placing faith in the American educational system, electoral politics, and their own claims to whiteness they could find middle-class success and distance themselves from their abused and persecuted forbears. Often they changed their names to sound more American and discouraged the use of Spanish. The ultimate goal of the Mexican-American Generation was to be classified as white. Later, Chicano activists, intensely proud of their cultural differences and indigenous past, were particularly scornful of this attitude, though many of them had grown up ingrained with the idea that white was right and that being Mexican was a source of shame.

Organizations formed to support Mexican Americanization, the most prominent of which was the League of United Latin American Citizens (LULAC), founded in Texas, in 1928. LULAC sought to protect Mexican Americans against segregation and mistreatment in the judicial system, but also to cultivate good citizenship and integration into mainstream society. Despite being critical of abuses, LULAC also promoted a belief that Mexican Americans had to change their ways if they were to ever gain full acceptance into

American society. The organization's official language was English, members had to be U.S. citizens, and whenever possible, LULAC advocated for Mexican Americans to be classified as white in census data and official records.

Youth groups also sprung up across the Southwest, such as the Mexican American Movement (MAM) in Southern California, which advocated for higher education and civic participation. Like LULAC, however, MAM also placed strong emphasis on self-improvement, not necessarily societal change, as the best means of advancement.

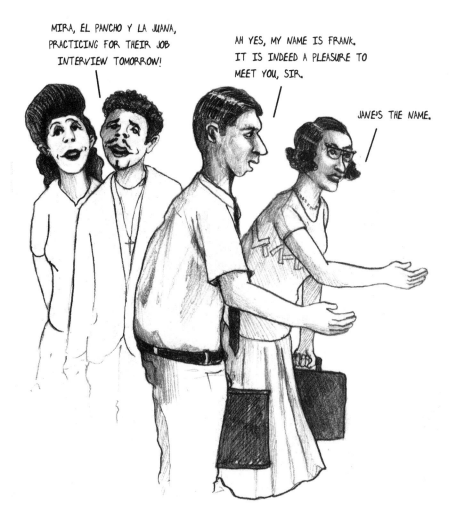

# THE LEMON GROVE INCIDENT AND SCHOOL DESEGREGATION

Long before *Brown v. Board of Education*, the landmark U.S. Supreme Court case that outlawed school segregation in 1954, Mexican Americans were at the center of school desegregation efforts. In San Diego, in 1930, the Lemon Grove School District attempted to create a separate school for Mexican and Mexican American students. A suit followed a year later, and the "Lemon Grove incident," as it was called, became the first successful desegregation court decision in the country. In the mid-1940s, in Orange County, *Mendez v. Westminster* again held that segregation of Mexican and Mexican American students was unconstitutional. Both cases are examples of the Mexican American community challenging racist practices and establishing important legal precedent, yet they have been largely relegated to historical footnotes.

During World War II, many Mexican Americans viewed service in the war effort as the ultimate demonstration of allegiance to the United States. Mexican Americans served in large numbers and won more Congressional Medals of Honor than any other minority group. Upon their return, however, they faced the same barriers to social and economic mobility. Mexican Americans were still segregated in schools, frequently barred from public facilities like swimming pools, restaurants and theaters, and discriminated against in the housing market. The American GI Forum was established in 1948 to protect the interests of returning Mexican American veterans, assisting

them in finding employment, access to housing, and gaining entry into college. In its first and most celebrated campaign, the GI Forum fought on behalf of Felix Longoria, a soldier who had been killed in the Philippines and was subsequently denied burial at a white-owned funeral home back in Texas. Because of the GI Forum's efforts, Longoria was eventually buried in Arlington National Cemetery.

Mexican Americans also had a long history of labor organizing, dating back to early vaqueros in the late 1800s and miners and agriculture workers in the early 1900s. During the Great Depression, agricultural labor organizing, especially in California, increased significantly, but it also met strong resistance from powerful growers. Violence, intimidation, and the threat of immigration raids were frequently used to break strikes. Union organizers were often accused of being Communists and un-American—further grounds for suppression.

Despite such opposing forces, Mexican Americans didn't back down. They routinely participated in efforts to demand fair treatment and wages in the workplace. One of the most famous acts of resistance was the Salt of the Earth Strike in New Mexico in 1950, led by women miners against the Empire Zinc Company. The strike became the subject of a famous 1954 film, *Salt of the Earth*, which brought an anti-communist backlash against the film's creators. Bert Corona and Ernesto Galarza were two of the most prominent labor organizers and community organizers whose efforts on behalf of workers and immigrants began in the late 1930s and continued through the Chicano Movement.

Although César Chávez gained national prominence in the 1960s for his efforts to start a union for farmworkers, it's important to note that he began organizing for the Community Service Organization (CSO), a Mexican American community organization, in the early 1950s, while he was still in his twenties. The CSO helped elect Edward R. Roybal, one of its co-founders, to the Los Angeles City Council in 1949, and to the U.S. House of Representatives in 1963.

The California-based Mexican American Political Association (MAPA), founded in 1959, and its Texas-based counterpart, the Political Association of Spanish-Speaking Organizations (PASSO), founded a year later, were formed to push for more political representation of Mexican Americans and to pressure the Democratic Party to recognize this important and growing minority. And during the presidential campaign of 1960, so-called Viva Kennedy! Clubs throughout the country gave young Mexican Americans their first taste of political activism.

Although the Mexican-American Generation was known for its assimilationist stance, many activists associated with the Chicano Movement, such as César Chávez and Rodolfo "Corky" Gonzalez, were part of that very generation. The beginning of the Chicano Movement is impossible to pinpoint, in part because efforts to fight for justice for the Mexican American community were ongoing for many years; they just took different forms and articulated their goals in different ways. For labor organizers it was about the bread-and-butter issues of fair wages and decent housing; for organizations like LULAC it was about ensuring Mexican Americans gained entry into the fabric of American life; and for the GI Forum it was about recognizing that Mexican American veterans had sacrificed their lives for their country and deserved to be honored rather than treated as second-class citizens.

Chicano activists were often critical of members from the Mexican-American Generation for their naïve belief that, if they just tried hard enough, American society would embrace them. And while it's true that they were far from articulating a radical vision of self-determination or cultural empowerment, the Chicano Movement also benefited from the groundwork they laid to organize, promote, and represent the Mexican American community.

## THE ZOOT SUITERS

Zoot suiters, or *pachucos,* as they called themselves, were a counter-culture Mexican American youth movement that blended a wide variety of cultural influences. The music they listened and danced to was a mix of Anglo-American, African American, Caribbean, and Mexican. Their dress—the zoot suit, or "drapes"—had origins in the black community. The slang they spoke, *caló,* was a mix of Spanish and English, but it was more complex than that; it included invented words and was rich in word play and rhyming schemes. Frequently

portrayed as dangerous outsiders, the zoot suiters were accused of speaking in code. In his famous (and in some ways infamous) essay, "The Pachuco and Other Extremes" (1953), the Mexican intellectual Octavio Paz describes pachucos as Mexican Americans who

DO NOT ATTEMPT TO VINDICATE THEIR RACE OR THE NATIONALITY OF THEIR FOREBEARS. THEIR ATTITUDE REVEALS AN OBSTINATE, ALMOST FANATICAL

WILL-TO-BE, BUT THIS WILL AFFIRMS NOTHING
SPECIFIC EXCEPT THEIR DETERMINATION – IT IS AN
AMBIGUOUS ONE, AS WE WILL SEE – NOT TO BE LIKE
THOSE AROUND THEM. THE PACHUCO DOES NOT WANT
TO BECOME A MEXICAN AGAIN; AT THE SAME TIME HE
DOES NOT WANT TO BLEND INTO THE LIFE OF NORTH
AMERICA.

Paz saw this "fanatical will-to-be" as a negative, rather than as a positive affirmation of a complex cultural identity.

Pachucos did not dismiss Mexican or North American culture just for the sake of it, but simply because they *weren't* Mexican like their forbearers; nor did they fit into the American mainstream mold. Instead, these young men and women created their own culture. They drew from multiple influences and, instead of hiding in the shadows or attempting to blend in, as many would have preferred them to do, they announced and flaunted their differences proudly. For that very reason, Chicano activists in the 1960s would celebrate the pachucos from the 1940s, regarding them as symbols of resistance and defiance in the face of two oppressive cultures.

At the time, however, many in mainstream American society and even in the Spanish-speaking community regarded zoot suiters as gang members or hoodlums. Mexican American youth in general were viewed as un-American—a heavy charge during wartime. The tension came to a head on June 3, 1943, when sailors on leave in Los Angeles, California, fought with a group of Mexican Americans wearing zoot suits. The following evening, some 200 sailors and Marines hired taxicabs to drive around the city looking for Mexican American teenagers. They attacked the ones they found, and they did so with impunity. The police refused to intervene. The following evening even more servicemen joined the hunt for zoot suiters. Left bloodied and broken, the Mexican American youth were the ones arrested and blamed for the violence. The newspapers joined in the cause, carrying headlines that portrayed the incidents as "riots" provoked by zoot suiters. By June 7, thousands of civilians had joined in the attacks on Mexican American youth, as well as blacks and Filipinos.

The police finally closed off downtown Los Angeles to servicemen, but the fighting continued elsewhere before finally subsiding. The indiscriminate nature of the beatings, the lack of police intervention except to arrest beaten Mexican Americans, and the media's role in whipping up anti-Mexican hysteria, left a deep wound in the Mexican American community. Although not all Mexicans or Mexican Americans identified with the pachucos—indeed many were critical of them—the so-called Zoot Suit Riots showed that animosity toward the Mexican American community was very real and that, pachuco or not, Mexicans from all walks of life were treated with suspicion and accused of disloyalty.

When later Chicano activists acknowledged the pachucos as their predecessors—the first Mexican American youth movement to establish an independent identity—they also remembered the violent response it provoked. Acceptance of Mexican Americans on their own terms was not going to happen without a fight.

## STACKED DECK

In 1960, one third of all Mexican American families lived below the poverty line and unemployment was twice that of whites. The jobs held by Mexican Americans were overwhelmingly unskilled or semiskilled—a third of them in agriculture or other difficult conditions. Mexican Americans attended segregated schools, where the curriculum ignored their history and culture and the use of Spanish was forbidden. There were hardly any Mexican American teachers. A staggering 75% of Mexican American students dropped out before finishing high school, usually to help support their families financially.

Mexican Americans also had very little political representation, not just in Congress and state legislatures, but also on school boards and city councils; and they were chronically underrepresented on juries. Wherever they turned, the deck was stacked against them. Racism and discrimination toward Mexican Americans was systemic, with little hope for change. As blacks in the South, led by Martin Luther King, Jr., and other civil rights activists, began to make gains and receive nationwide attention for their plight, Mexican American attitudes began to change as well. They recognized that they didn't have to disappear or blend into white America in order to improve their conditions. They saw African Americans finally standing up for their rights and doing so with pride, with conviction. Now it was their turn.

# 2

## FINDING INSPIRATION

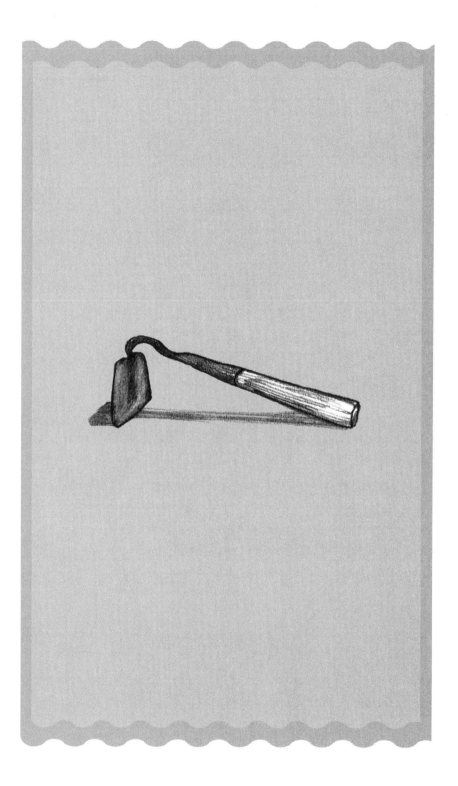

# CÉSAR CHÁVEZ, DOLORES HUERTA, AND THE ORGANIZER'S TALE

In 1965, the National Farm Workers Association (NFWA) began a defining strike against the powerful growers in Delano, California. Led by César Chávez and Dolores Huerta, the walkout sought to improve deplorable working conditions in the fields, labor that left bodies broken, and pay that kept families mired in cyclical poverty. The farmworkers were the Mexican American community's most

vulnerable population. They worked long hours for meager wages and were treated as expendable; there was always another desperate worker willing to work for less. By the time the farmworker strike gained national attention, most Mexican Americans had left the fields and were concentrated in urban centers, but many still retained a strong connection to their agricultural roots.

*La Causa*—"the cause," as the farmworkers' quest for unionization became known—was an important inspiration to Mexican Americans everywhere because they closely identified with the strikers; they saw themselves, or their parents, or their grandparents. If the poorest and most exploited of the Mexican American community could rise up and demand their rights in the face of brutal oppression, then so could they. The farmworker struggle, though only one part of the Chicano Movement, was its emotional core and provided its most enduring symbols.

## CÉSAR CHÁVEZ

César Chávez remains the most well-known of the Chicano Movement leaders, and he was the first to gain nationwide attention. He was seen as the Mexican American Martin Luther King, Jr., and the comparison went beyond the superficial. Chávez drew heavily on King's philosophy of nonviolence as the best means of enacting change.

Born in 1927 in the North Gila Valley of Arizona, Chávez was the second of five children. His parents lost their farm during the Great Depression, and the family was forced to become migrant farmworkers in order to survive. They followed the harvest to California, lived in squalid labor camps, and Chávez dropped out of school in the eighth grade to work full time in the fields. The hardships his family experienced sensitized Chávez to the suffering endured by all migrant farmworkers. He served for two years in the U.S. Navy (1946–1948) and, upon completing his service, married his high school girlfriend, Helen Fabela. The couple had eight children, and Helen would be an important ally in her husband's organizing activities.

Chávez got his start as an organizer in 1950 with a Mexican

American advocacy group called the Community Service Organization (CSO), led by Fred Ross. Sent door-to-door to register voters and gain support for different campaigns, Chávez was so effective that he rose quickly up the ranks of the CSO; by 1960 he had become national director. He eventually grew disenchanted with the CSO's unwillingness to organize agricultural workers, so in 1962 he left the group and moved to Delano to organize farmworkers. He convinced fellow CSO organizers Gilberto Padilla and Dolores Huerta to join him, and together they established the National Farm Workers Association (NFWA).

BRACEROS

## DOLORES HUERTA

An effective lobbyist and articulate spokeswoman from the outset, Dolores Huerta was one of the co-founders of the farmworkers union, serving as its main negotiator and later as vice president. Unlike most of the union leadership, Dolores Huerta didn't grow up working in the fields. She was born on April 10, 1930, in the mountains of northern New Mexico; her father was a farmworker, miner, and union activist who also served in the New Mexico state legislature. When her parents divorced, Huerta moved with her mother to Stockton, California, where her mother ran a restaurant and a hotel and was an active participant in the church and community life. Huerta studied to become a teacher and, by her own admission, was following the path to a comfortable middle-class life in the suburbs. But she couldn't turn away from the poverty she saw all around her.

Much like Chávez, Huerta was recruited by Fred Ross to work with the CSO and soon distinguished herself by her tireless advocacy and lobbying skills on issues such as disability insurance, pension and public-assistance programs, and the right to vote in Spanish. One of Huerta's and the CSO's successful lobbying efforts was to help end the Bracero Program, which was established to make up for labor shortages during World War II, but in subsequent years had become a vehicle for growers to hire cheap, easily exploitable labor. Despite all their efforts and success, by the time Chávez and Huerta both departed the CSO, they did so believing that many of their colleagues in the organization were self-seeking professionals who lacked the urgency required to represent a population whose extreme exploitation and vulnerability made them particularly difficult to organize. As such, the NFWA was established on the principle that it would require great sacrifice not just of its members but also of its leaders. For the next decade, Chávez and Huerta became the face of that sacrifice.

## THE ORGANIZER'S TALE

Based on their grassroots experience with the CSO, Chávez and his fellow organizers began their efforts with the NFWA by going door-to-door. It was slow going. In a 1966 magazine article titled "The Organizer's Tale," Chávez wrote,

> FOR SIX MONTHS I TRAVELED AROUND, PLANTING AN IDEA. WE HAD A SIMPLE QUESTIONNAIRE, A LITTLE CARD WITH SPACE FOR NAME, ADDRESS, AND HOW MUCH THE WORKER THOUGHT HE OUGHT TO BE PAID... SOME EIGHTY THOUSAND CARDS WERE SENT BACK FROM EIGHT VALLEY COUNTIES...SOMETIMES PEOPLE SCRIBBLED MESSAGES ON THE CARDS: 'I HOPE TO GOD WE WIN' OR 'DO YOU THINK WE CAN WIN?' OR 'I'D LIKE TO KNOW MORE.' SO I SEPARATED THE CARDS WITH THE PENCILED NOTES, GOT IN MY CAR, AND WENT TO THOSE PEOPLE.
>
> *RAMPARTS*, JULY 1966

Wanting to remain autonomous and build from the ground up, the union refused outside donations. As a result, Chávez predicted that it would take many years before the union had the numbers and the coffers to undertake any significant action.

By 1964, the union had a few hundred members, an insurance program, and a credit union, as well as a newspaper, called *El Malcriado*. It held its first successful strike in May 1965 on behalf of rose grafters in McFarland, California, resulting in higher wages for the workers. This was followed by another successful strike against Martin Farms, a small grape grower in the state. Although these efforts were encouraging and provided valuable experience, they failed to reach the union's ultimate goal: recognition of the NFWA as the workers'

legal collective bargaining agent. Still, they paved the way for the challenge that lay ahead.

In the summer of 1965, another union seeking to represent California farmworkers, the Agricultural Workers Organizing Committee (AWOC), organized a series of walkout strikes among predominantly Filipino grape laborers led by organizer Larry Itliong. Again, the walkouts resulted in wage increases but failed to achieve a collective bargaining contract. Realizing that AWOC's strikes were going to be hamstrung as long as Mexican and Mexican American workers continued to work, Itliong approached Chávez about joining the strike. Chávez was reluctant, feeling that his union needed more time to grow and become financially secure, but he didn't feel right about keeping NFWA workers in the fields while other farm laborers were on strike. So he put the issue to a vote, and on September 16, 1965, Mexican Independence Day, the now 1,200-member NFWA joined the strike against two of California's largest growers, Schenley Industries and the DiGiorgio Fruit Corporation. Shortly thereafter, a boycott was called on grapes grown by Schenley, DiGiorgio, and 83 other wine growers.

# UNSUNG HERO: LARRY ITLIONG

Although Larry Itliong was the labor leader who invited César Chávez and the NFWA to join AWOC and its mainly Filipino membership in the grape strike, his role has been largely forgotten by history. So, too, has the important alliance between Filipino and Mexican laborers. The two groups of workers had long been pitted against one another in order to undercut each other's wages, and Itliong knew that their efforts would not be successful if they went at it alone. The merging of the two unions created a stronger base from which to organize and negotiate, but it also pushed Itliong into a backseat role. In 1971, frustrated with the union's direction, including its lack of focus

LARRY ITLIONG

on Filipino worker issues, Itliong left the United Farm Workers. Though he continued to advocate for Filipino American fieldworkers until his death in 1977, Itliong and other Filipino American labor leaders such a Philip Vera Cruz remained largely unrecognized in accounts of the farmworker movement. To help correct the oversight, the State of California in 2015 established October 25 as Larry Itliong Day.

The union met fierce, often violent resistance. The growers brought in scabs—strikebreakers, many of them undocumented Mexican immigrants—to work the fields. When strikers tried to prevent scabs from crossing the picket line, or when they stood nearby and tried to convince them to walk off the job, the growers' henchmen attacked. Often the police intervened to intimidate the strikers, break up the protests, or outright arrest them. Chávez and other union organizers were frequently accused of being Communists in order to dissuade the public from supporting their cause.

The growers were powerful as well as rich, backed by the political establishment and law enforcement. Also on their side was the indifference of American society at large. Few knew of the horrible conditions in the fields and labor camps, and few questioned where their produce came from or who grew it. Chávez and the UFWA realized that as long as it was the powerless

DON'T BE AN ESQUIROL!

HUELGA

ESQUIROL = SCAB = STRIKE BREAKER

MARCH FROM DELANO TO SACRAMENTO - 1966

fighting the powerful growers (and on the growers' own turf) they were fighting a lost cause. They had to raise awareness of their plight, and in order to do so they needed new tactics.

## THE PILGRIMAGE

In the spring of 1966, Chávez asked for a hearing before the U.S. Senate Migratory Subcommittee to air the workers' grievances. The committee met that March in Delano, where Chávez struck a bond with its most influential member, Senator Robert Kennedy. The New

York legislator became an ardent defender of the farmworker cause, castigating the strong-armed tactics used by growers and local law enforcement. His support boosted the morale of the strikers and media coverage of their cause. Viewers across the country tuned in to watch nightly news reports on the subcommittee hearings.

With the eyes of the country on Delano, Chávez and the NFWA embarked on a new plan to win the battle of public opinion. Inspired by the nonviolent marches employed by Martin Luther King, Jr., and the Southern Christian Leadership Conference in the South, Chávez decided that the NFWA and its supporters would march from Delano to the state capitol in Sacramento, a 250-mile journey. The march took 21 days and grew in number with every rural town it met along the way. The outpouring demonstrated to the public that the union had the support of rank-and-file workers, countering grower claims that Chávez and the NFWA were outside Communist agitators.

Especially sensitive to that charge, Chávez was careful to present the farmworkers' plight not in political terms—i.e., as a fight against capitalism—but as a spiritual battle. The march, cast more as a pilgrimage, was part of that effort. Mass was given daily, and the marchers invoked the Virgin of Guadalupe, the patron saint of Mexico, as their protector. At the head of the crowd, a flag bearing the image of the Virgin of Guadalupe guided the way. "De Colores," a song with religious origins, was the union's theme song. In the "Plan of Delano," the marcher's manifesto, the farmworkers' plight is depicted in biblical terms, the weak fighting the strong. Chávez was an observant Catholic, as were most of his farmworker supporters, so the sentiment was genuine, but he was also conscious that the American public was paying close attention and that its sympathies were essential to the farmworkers' larger cause.

## THE PLAN OF DELANO

The first of many important Chicano Movement manifestos, the Plan of Delano was drafted by Luis Valdez, a recent graduate of San José State College and budding playwright who sought to use *teatro,* or theater, as an organizing tool in the farmworker struggle. The Plan was a proclamation to the world that laid out the goals of the marchers and their plight. There was something in it for everyone.

For the pious: "All men are brothers, sons of the same God; that is why we say to all men of good will, in the words of Pope Leo XII, 'Everyone's first duty is to protect the workers from the greed of speculators who use human beings as instruments to provide themselves with money.'"

For the radical: "We shall pursue the REVOLUTION we have proposed. We are sons of the Mexican Revolution, a revolution of the poor seeking bread and justice. Our revolution will not be armed, but we want the existing social order to dissolve; we want a new social order."

For those who understood the historical significance of the pilgrimage and found support in the U.S. Bill of Rights and the American Revolutionary spirit: "We seek our basic, God-given rights as human beings. Because we have suffered—and are not afraid to suffer—in order to survive, we are ready to give up everything, even our lives, in our fight for social justice."

And for those who recognized the farmworkers' struggle not just as a labor issue, but as a larger social movement—like the fight for civil rights in the South, another test of the country's soul: "We know that the poverty of the Mexican or Filipino worker in California is the same as that of all farm workers across the country, the Negroes and poor whites, the Puerto Ricans, Japanese, and Arabians; in short, all of the races that comprise the oppressed minorities of the United States."

As the farmworker strike gained national attention, it also attracted the sympathies of young Mexican Americans, many of whom were becoming increasingly radicalized by the Civil Rights Movement and the dramatic social changes happening in the rest of the country. The pilgrimage and the Plan of Delano helped them realize that they had a cause of their own to support. It wasn't long before *La Huelga*, the strike, transformed into *La Causa*, the cause that would further inspire the Chicano Movement.

## EL MALCRIADO

First published in 1964, *El Malcriado* was the official organ of the National Farm Workers Association. Meaning "ill-bred" or "mischievous," *El Malcriado* was originally published exclusively in Spanish and distributed among farmworkers in the Delano area in order to raise awareness about local labor issues and the union's efforts. Later it was published in English and increased its readership to a national audience. Among the most memorable

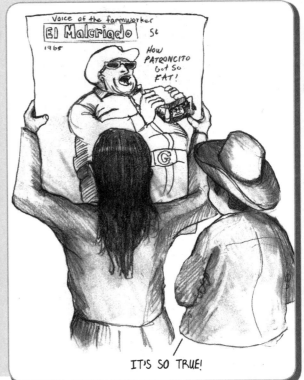

features of the newspaper were cartoons that employed humor and satire to address worker exploitation. Many of them depicted Don Sotaco, a character developed by artist Andrew Zermeño, as he battled the evil Don Coyote, a manipulative contractor, and the rotund Patroncito, who grew fat feeding off farmworker labor. *El Malcriado* became an example for subsequent Chicano Movement newspapers that combined political commentary, biting humor, and innovative artwork to appeal to as wide an audience as possible.

## EL TEATRO CAMPESINO

El Teatro Campesino, or the farmworkers' theater, was the first example of fledgling Chicano activists joining forces with the farmworker struggle. Founder Luis Valdez pitched the idea to Chávez himself, who was supportive but warned that there would be no funding available, no actors, no stage, and not even time to rehearse because of the strike. Valdez was undeterred. Having performed with the San Francisco Mime Troupe, a guerrilla theater company, he believed that theater should respond to and grow out of the social conditions where it was most necessary—in this case the picket line. Valdez and other teatro members wrote one-act plays called *actos,* which had roots in agitprop theater and early Mexican *carpas,* or tent acts, which employed humor and the absurd.

The actos spoke directly to issues facing the farmworkers. In perhaps its best-known example, *Las Dos Caras del Patroncito (Two Faces of the Boss),* Teatro Campesino dramatized the willingness of farmworkers to believe the growers' paternal attitude. In the play, the boss character tries to convince a recently arrived Mexican strikebreaker that *he's* the one who has it hard: "You've got it good! Now look at

NOW IT MAKES COMPLETE SENSE!

me, they say I'm greedy, that I'm rich. Well, let me tell you, boy, I got problems. No free housing for me, Pancho. I gotta pay for what I got." Eventually the roles are reversed, as characters change masks and the farmworker becomes the boss. In doing so, he gains confidence and starts ordering the boss around. Now, living in the farmworker's shoes, the boss ends up calling out for help from Chávez and his union.

Inventive and entertaining, Teatro Campesino intended for the actos' message to be direct. Its audience, most of whom had never experienced live theater, could easily identify the heroes and villains and could clearly understand the issue at hand. Performed throughout the march from Delano to Sacramento, often on the back of flatbed trucks, the shows became an effective organizing tool. In Valdez's words, Teatro Campesino

IS TAKING FROM THE OLD AND CREATING THE NEW. IT IS PUTTING ALL THE JOYS, SORROWS, HISTORY, AND CULTURE OF LA RAZA ON STAGE TO BE EXAMINED, TO BE REMADE, TO PASS ON TO OTHERS AND TO SHOW OTHERS THAT THERE ARE ANSWERS, THAT THINGS DON'T HAVE TO BE THIS WAY.

Teatro Campesino was also the first demonstration of the important role that the arts could play in developing political consciousness. Soon other art forms, such as murals, posters, and songs, would be used to support the burgeoning movement.

## SYMBOLS OF THE HUELGA

As the farmworker strike gained nationwide attention, César Chávez became more and more of a civil rights icon. Short in stature, plainly dressed, and with a gold-capped tooth, he didn't look the part. He was also soft-spoken, lacking the soaring oratory of Martin Luther King, Jr., and Malcolm X, or the fiery rhetoric of other Chicano Movement leaders popping up around the country. In a way this served his cause. He projected the image of a humble man representing a humble people who sought no more than a life lived with dignity. Even as other activists became increasingly radicalized, calling for greater change and societal upheaval, Chávez remained a symbol of righteousness and perseverance.

Other symbols of the farmworker struggle found their way into the lexicon and imagery of Chicano activism. The terms *La Causa*

BOYCOTT GRAPES!
¡Qué viva la HUELGA!

SYMBOLS OF
LA HUELGA

EL PICKET SIGN

UFW FLAG

("the cause") and *Huelga* ("strike") both came to signify struggle in general. Union rallies frequently included chants of *¡Qué viva la Huelga!* ("Long Live the Strike!") and *¡Qué viva la Causa!* ("Long Live the Cause!"). The farmworkers union adopted the slogan, *¡Sí, se puede!* ("Yes, we can!"), which took on a meaning greater than just union activism. Even more significant was the red farmworker flag and its emblem, a black eagle. Carried by marchers on the pilgrimage to Sacramento, visible at every protest, picket line, and union meeting, the farmworker eagle became the most powerful symbol of the Chicano Movement. As Chávez explained in "The Organizer's Tale," the flag's effectiveness didn't happen by accident:

> I WANTED DESPERATELY TO GET SOME COLOR INTO THE MOVEMENT, TO GIVE PEOPLE SOMETHING THEY COULD IDENTIFY WITH, LIKE A FLAG. I WAS READING SOME BOOKS ABOUT HOW VARIOUS LEADERS DISCOVERED WHAT COLORS CONTRASTED AND STOOD OUT BEST. THE EGYPTIANS HAD FOUND THAT A RED

BOYCOTT GRAPES

GIUMARRA GRAPES *are* SCAB GRAPES

THE GRAPE BOYCOTT SPREADS ACROSS THE COUNTRY.

FIELD WITH A WHITE CIRCLE AND A BLACK EMBLEM IN THE CENTER CRASHED INTO YOUR EYES LIKE NOTHING ELSE. I WANTED TO USE THE AZTEC EAGLE IN THE CENTER, AS ON THE MEXICAN FLAG. SO I TOLD MY COUSIN MANUEL, 'DRAW AN AZTEC EAGLE.' MANUEL HAD A LITTLE TROUBLE WITH IT, SO WE MODIFIED THE EAGLE TO MAKE IT EASIER FOR PEOPLE TO DRAW.

The farmworker eagle first appeared on flags, picket signs and leaflets, then Chicano artists began using it in posters and murals, and before long it had become an immediate signifier for the Mexican American civil rights struggle.

# THE GRAPE BOYCOTT

In April 1966, shortly before the end of the pilgrimage, Schenley Industries called to negotiate a contract. They would submit to all the union's demands. By the time the marchers reached Sacramento, other wine grape producers, including Gallo and Franzia Brothers, had also signed contracts. Later that summer, in an effort to strengthen its hand, the NFWA officially merged with Larry Itliong's AWOC to form the United Farm Workers Organizing Committee (UFWOC), resulting in less autonomy for the farmworkers union, but greater numbers and resources. The DiGiorgio Corporation would soon capitulate to worker demands as well, but not before trying to undercut the UFWOC's efforts by negotiating with the more accommodating Teamsters Union. As its successes mounted, the UFWOC was all too aware that greater challenges lay ahead, including the biggest table grape grower of them all, the Giumarra Vineyards Corporation, which remained steadfast in its opposition to unionization.

A nationwide boycott was called on Giumarra grapes, and many union organizers were sent to cities across the country to organize boycott meetings and fundraising events. Giumarra quickly sought to undermine the boycott by illegally using the labels of other grape companies. In response, the UFWOC called for a boycott of *all* table grapes. The boycott effort brought the farmworker struggle directly into Americans' daily lives. At supermarkets, picketers sporting signs and distributing leaflets urged shoppers to avoid table grapes. Sometimes the boycotters were more disruptive and outright intimidated shoppers to keep them away. Student protestors and Chicano activists across the country picked up the boycott efforts and were essential in increasing the union's clout. Among them were young organizers like Eliseo Medina, who got his start coordinating boycott activities in Chicago.

Other unions and religious organizations also pledged support for the boycott. Supermarkets began cancelling orders for grapes, sometimes out of sympathy for the cause but often because they tired of the disruption and negative publicity. Despite these small gains, however, political power remained on the side of the growers. California governor Ronald Reagan snubbed his nose at the boycott and proceeded to snack publicly on grapes, and President Richard Nixon tripled orders for grapes sent to U.S. troops in Vietnam. Growers were still able to find an almost limitless supply of strikebreakers from Mexico and, much to the dismay of the farmworkers union, in fall of 1967, the entire California table grape crop was harvested.

ICONIC IMAGE: CESAR CHAVEZ
BREAKING HIS FAST WITH BOBBY KENNEDY

With the strike dragging on, resources dwindling, and morale low, many union members called for more extreme tactics, including the use of violence and sabotage. Chávez continued to insist on nonviolence, but many of his supporters were losing patience and violent incidents increased. In the spring of 1968, inspired by the example of the Indian leader Mahatma Gandhi, Chávez decided to go on a hunger strike to demonstrate his sacrifice for the cause and to quell unrest in the ranks of the union. Many unionists were critical, not understanding what the fast had to do with the strike or how it furthered the farmworker movement. But Chávez's hunger strike, which lasted for 25 days, became an important symbol and burnished his image as a civil rights hero. Around the country,

ICONIC IMAGE:
DOLORES HOLDING
HUELGA SIGN.

people stopped eating table grapes in a show of solidarity. The boycott effort was reenergized.

Senator Robert Kennedy, shortly before his assassination in Los Angeles on June 6, joined Chávez on the last day of his fast. The two took Communion together, resulting in one of the lasting images of the Chicano Movement. Kennedy called Chávez "one of the heroic figures of our time." Chávez, having lost 35 pounds and too weak to speak, had someone read the following words on his behalf:

> IT IS HOW WE USE OUR LIVES THAT DETERMINES WHAT KIND OF MEN WE ARE. . . . I AM CONVINCED THAT THE TRUEST ACT OF COURAGE, THE STRONGEST ACT OF MANLINESS, IS TO SACRIFICE OURSELVES FOR OTHERS IN A TOTALLY NONVIOLENT STRUGGLE FOR JUSTICE. TO BE A MAN IS TO SUFFER FOR OTHERS. GOD HELP US BE MEN.

# UNSUNG HERO: JESSE DE LA CRUZ

The UFW's first female recruiter, Jesse de la Cruz, was one of the leaders of the farmworkers' movement often overshadowed by the focus on César Chávez and Dolores Huerta. As depicted in a 1998 TV miniseries about women's labor movements titled *A Will of Their Own*, as well as a 2000 biography by author Gary Soto, de la Cruz was a lifelong farm-worker, a mother of six, and already in her forties when she came into contact with the union. Her husband had invited Chávez to hold meetings at their home. De la Cruz was in the kitchen when Chávez encouraged her to come out and join the conversation. She was soon working as an organizer. Traveling around the Fresno area, she became one of the most effective recruiters in the farmworkers union. She later helped efforts to ban the short handled hoe (a hand tool that led to debilitating back injuries), taught English to migrant workers, and served as a delegate to the 1972 Democratic National Convention.

The fight would continue for two more years. In the spring of 1970, Lionel Steinberg, the owner of Freedman Farms, signed a contract with the farmworkers union and a union label was placed on his table grape crates. Stores now sold Freedman Farms grapes, which commanded higher prices. It wasn't long before other grape growers, tired of their fruit rotting in warehouses, signed similar contracts and received the now coveted union label. Finally, John

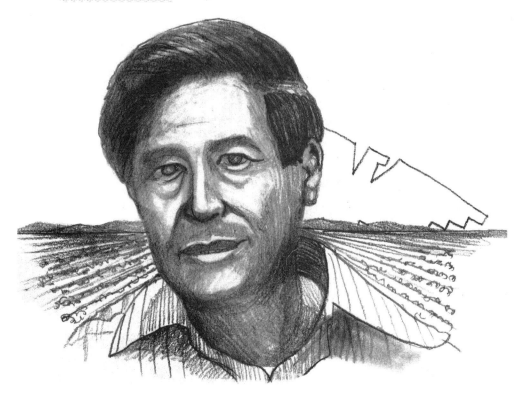

Giumarra, Sr., the owner of Giumarra Farms who had repeatedly accused Chávez and the union of being "reds," agreed to a contract. The union, however, held out until Giumarra could bring all table grape companies to the negotiating table. On July 29, 1970, five years after the strike began, Dolores Huerta negotiated a settlement with the table grape growers that provided higher wages and benefits for scores of workers, ending the most successful consumer boycott in labor history.

Momentum was clearly on the side of the farmworkers, but the struggle was far from over. On Labor Day (September 1) 1970, just over a month after the Giumarra contract was signed, Chávez called for a strike against lettuce growers in Salinas, California. The union faced an uphill battle, as growers were prepared and found ways of undermining its efforts. Chávez was jailed for violating a court-issued injunction, and the Teamsters Union signed "sweetheart" deals with the growers that benefited growers over workers.

As the years progressed, Chávez found it difficult to transform what was a successful social movement into a nationwide labor organization that could deliver on the bread-and-butter issues needed by farmworkers. Finding roadblocks at every turn, the union eventually lost many of its most important contracts. Nevertheless, the efforts of the UFWOC—which was renamed the United Farm Workers (UFW) in 1972—increased wages for agricultural laborers and secured them health care benefits, disability insurance, pensions plans, and formal channels for airing grievances. The crippling short hoe, which forced workers to work stooped over, was eliminated, as were many dangerous pesticides. In 1975, the UFW helped usher in the Agricultural Labor Relations Act, ensuring protection for farmworkers in labor negotiations; many consider that legislation the union's crowning achievement.

Despite later setbacks, the farmworkers' struggle was a foundation for the Chicano Movement. César Chávez and Dolores Huerta became Chicano icons, and Chicano activists who worked with the unionists were able to employ similar grassroots tactics for causes such as school reform, political campaigns, and community self-determination. Not least, the farmworker struggle showed the Mexican American community that it was possible to stand up against injustice and dare to win.

# 3

## THE MOVEMENT SPREADS

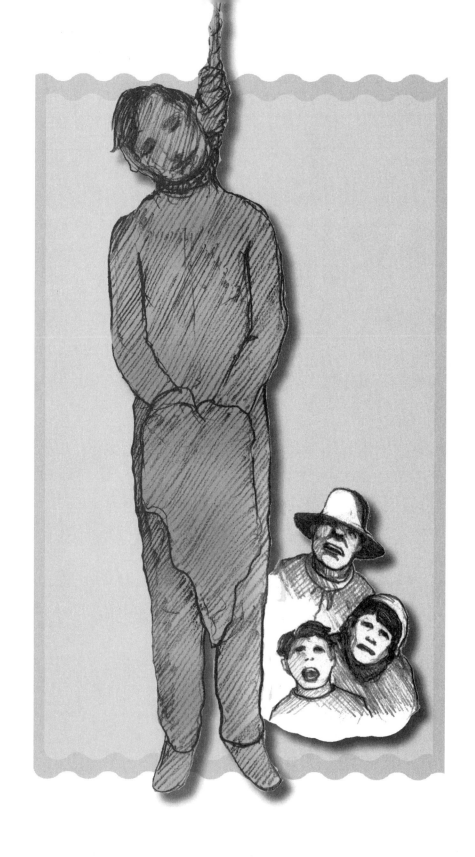

# REIES LÓPEZ TIJERINA AND THE LAND GRANT MOVEMENT

In the early 1960s, activist and former evangelist Reies López Tijerina established the Alianza Federál de Mercedes Reales in New Mexico. The Alianza, as it was known, sought to reclaim the land grants that were stripped away following the Mexican-American War and the Treaty of Guadalupe Hidalgo in 1848. Tijerina was a firebrand and one of the most controversial figures of the Chicano Movement. On the surface, Tijerina and César Chávez appear to be a study in contrasts. Whereas Chávez and the UFW preached nonviolence, Tijerina's tactics were notably more aggressive. But the two men shared many similarities. Both possessed a deep spiritual (some have said messianic) belief in their struggle, and many of their actions were intended symbolically as they sought to bring attention to their long-ignored causes.

An electrifying speaker, Tijerina inspired Mexican Americans across the country with his willingness to defy the status quo. The first to point out that the Mexican American community had been systematically disenfranchised, Tijerina raised awareness that Mexican Americans—or "Indo-Hispanos" as he preferred to call his New Mexican followers—were in their homeland and that they had a right to reclaim it. In 1967, Tijerina and the Alianza burst onto the national stage when he attempted to carry out a raid on the county courthouse in Tierra Amarilla, New Mexico. Although the raid was bungled in every sense, the ensuing manhunt spotlighted an individual who wasn't afraid of challenging the entrenched authority.

Reies López Tijerina was born September 21, 1926, near Falls City, Texas. His parents were sharecroppers, and as a boy Tijerina worked the fields alongside them. The family lived in extreme poverty and experienced harsh living conditions in a region known for

TIJERINA THE
EVANGELIST

its virulent racism. Among the strong influences on Tijerina's development no doubt were the stories about his great-grandfather, who
was hanged by Texas Rangers while his family looked on, and about
his grandfather, who in turn became a border raider who terrorized
Anglo ranchers and settlers. Tijerina had only a few years of school-
ing but taught himself how to read and write in both English and
Spanish. Converted by a Baptist missionary at the age of 15, he later
attended the Assemblies of God Bible School in Ysleta, Texas. He
was expelled for being found unchaperoned with a female student,
but his deep faith and natural oratory skills led him to become a

Pentecostal preacher. In his role as an evangelist, Tijerina, along with his first wife Maria, traveled around the country proselytizing an ascetic lifestyle.

In 1955, Tijerina, frustrated with the church's lack of commitment to the poor, distanced himself from organized Christianity and established a utopian commune in a remote Arizona desert that he named Valle de Paz (Valley of Peace), where some 20 families lived in makeshift earthen homes. His daughter, the first child born in the community, was named Ira de Alá (Wrath of God), a reflection of Tijerina's disillusionment with greater society. Modeled after the first-century Christian church, the commune was short-lived. It suffered not only in the face of the elements but was harassed by Anglo ranchers, and eventually vandals, who destroyed the dugout homes,

WAIT, WHERE ARE WE GOING?

TIJERINA LEADING HIS FOLLOWERS TO THE VALLEY OF PEACE

church, and schoolhouse. Ultimately, local authorities intervened to force the children of Valle de Paz to attend public schools, which the community refused despite mounting pressure. With the commune's financial situation deteriorating, and after repeated run-ins with the law, Tijerina was forced to flee Arizona and take his utopian dreams with him.

He spent years on the move, including an extended stay in Mexico. It was during that time that he studied centuries of colonial documents, including Spanish and Mexican land grants, legal texts, and the Treaty of Guadalupe Hidalgo. Tijerina had always been a strong follower of dreams and visions, and in 1956 he'd had a mysterious dream that he believed pointed him to a higher cause. Unsure of its significance at the time, he became convinced that his mission was to recover ancestral lands on behalf of the New Mexican descendants of the original grantees.

Upon his return to New Mexico, Tijerina found a population of increasingly embittered Mexican Americans who lived in dire poverty and were repeatedly pushed off land that had been theirs for generations. Many were ready to share his vision. Tijerina reconverted to Roman Catholicism in 1961, and, following his divorce in 1963, married his second wife, Patsy Romero, a native of Tierra Amarilla and a land grant heir. Spanish-speaking New Mexicans increasingly saw him as one of their own.

# LAS GORRAS BLANCAS AND LA MANO NEGRA

IT'S NOT WHAT IT LOOKS LIKE.

LAS GORRAS BLANCAS

Reies López Tijerina was certainly not the first to resist Anglo American seizure of Mexican American lands in New Mexico. In the 1890s, a group called *Las Gorras Blancas* (The White Caps) went on night raids, burning buildings, tearing down fences, and derailing trains to dissuade Anglo land developers and railroad companies from seizing more of their property. A secret organization called *La Mano Negra* (The Black Hand) sprang up later and performed similar acts of resistance into the late 1920s.

# LAND GRANTS AND LA ALIANZA

The Treaty of Guadalupe Hidalgo, which ended the Mexican-American War in 1848, guaranteed Mexicans who remained in the United States the full protection of the law and rights to their property, including Spanish and Mexican land grants. Shortly thereafter, however, the United States, not wanting large tracts of land to be off limits to Anglo colonizers, effectively removed the land-grant provision. Not yet a state, New Mexico had no recourse to influence the way land grants claims were handled. As a result, countless loopholes were exploited and millions of acres were stripped from their Mexican American owners and awarded to Anglo speculators. Within 50 years of the conflict, Spanish-speaking New Mexicans had lost 80% of their landholdings.

The Mexican American community suffered greatly from the dispossession for at least a century. Many Spanish-speaking New Mexicans were forced to migrate in order to survive, and those that remained saw their lands further encroached upon. The double standards shown to Mexican Americans were humiliating. As one example, the U.S. Forest Service banned access to grazing lands that their families had used for centuries, while granting permits to Anglo ranchers.

Reies López Tijerina, using his knowledge of the land grants and treaties, as well as his personal magnetism, organized Spanish-speaking New Mexicans to demand that the U.S. government respect the Treaty of Guadalupe Hidalgo. Though land rights were the main issue, Tijerina also cultivated ideas of Indo-Hispano cultural pride centered on language and history. In addition, he called for justice in the legal system, bilingual education, and economic equality. To promote his cause, he founded the Alianza Federál de Mercedes Reales, or the Federal Alliance of Land Grants, in 1963. Within a few short years, the organization boasted 20,000 members. The Alianza was extremely active, with Alianzistas, as they were called, holding annual conferences as well as frequent protests and marches. They publicized their views in the media, including a daily radio show called "The Voice of Justice" in which Tijerina lambasted the Anglo establishment for its mistreatment of Mexican Americans. The Alianza also actively pursued its claims in court, believing that the land claims were valid and that eventually the legal process would prevail. But the movement would soon gain notoriety for its more unconventional tactics.

## THE SANTA FE MARCH AND REPUBLIC OF SAN JOAQUÍN DEL RÍO DE CHAMA

Inspired by the African American civil rights marches in the South and by César Chávez's farmworker pilgrimage from Delano to Sacramento, Tijerina and the Alianza on July 4, 1966, embarked on a 66 mile march from Albuquerque to Santa Fe. Led by an old man astride a donkey carrying a flag representing the Tierra Amarilla land grant, the 300 marchers made it to Sante Fe in three days. They camped on the outskirts of the city while waiting for Governor Jack Campbell, who was out of state at the time. Upon his return, the governor met with Tijerina and agreed to investigate the land grant issue.

After three months without a response, the Alianza took more dramatic action, proclaiming that 500,000 acres of the U.S. Kit

Carson National Forest would be returned to the heirs of the original land grantees. Going a step further, the protesters declared the land a sovereign city-state called the Republic of San Joaquín del Río de Chama. Over 300 members of the Alianza, in a caravan of honking cars, stormed the national forest and occupied the Echo Amphitheater campground. When Forest Service rangers attempted to collect the entrance fees, the confrontation escalated. The Alianzistas arrested the rangers and placed them on trial for trespassing on the new republic. The incident was more theater than actual secession (apparently, tourist visas were issued to park visitors); the rangers were soon released, and days later the Alianzistas were removed from the camp under a court order. Political theater or not, Chicano activists viewed the Alianza takeover in nationalistic

terms: the reclaiming of a homeland, and not just figuratively. The incident represented a radical turn in tactics and expanded the possibilities for Chicano activism.

## TIERRA AMARILLA COURTHOUSE RAID

In the months that followed, state authorities—most notably District Attorney Alfonso Sánchez—persisted in harassing Tijerina, who had been arrested after the Echo Amphitheater incident and released on bail. Acts of arson and vandalism were attributed to Alianzistas throughout northern New Mexico. After District Attorney Sánchez sought to obtain the Alianza membership list, Tijerina resigned and dissolved the organization. Members reconstituted themselves as Alianza Federál de Pueblos Libres (The Federal Alliance of Free

City-States), but it wasn't long before pressure from authorities forced Tijerina to go into hiding. Hearing word that Alianzistas were going to congregate in the town of Coyote, District Attorney Sánchez threatened to arrest Alianza members for unlawful assembly. Road blockades were set up, homes were raided, and 11 members were arrested.

With the meeting in Coyote thwarted, Tijerina met with members a few days later in the town of Canjilón. When they heard over the radio that Sánchez was scheduled to appear in the Rio Arriba County Courthouse in Tierra Amarilla to formally charge the 11 Alianzistas who had been arrested, Tijerina decided to go on the offensive. On June 5, 1967, he and 20 other men, along with his oldest daughter Rose, headed to Tierra Amarilla to free the prisoners and make a citizen's arrest of District Attorney Sánchez. Later Tijerina would write,

THE PRESS DUBBED ME 'KING TIGER.'

I FELT THAT MY DUTY WAS TO PROVIDE AN EXAMPLE OF VALOR TO THE PEOPLE. THE ANGLO WANTED TO SQUASH ME SO I COULD NOT AWAKEN THE PEOPLE. I HAD KNOWN THIS EVER SINCE I BEGAN TO FIGHT FOR THE LAND IN 1956. I FELT THAT THIS WAS THE MOMENT OF DECISION IN THE STRUGGLE AGAINST THOSE WHO HAD ROBBED MY PEOPLE OF THEIR LAND AND CULTURE.

Despite his grand intentions, the courthouse raid went disastrously wrong. After storming the building, the armed men discovered that Sánchez was not even there. In the ensuing gunfire, a state patrolman and a jailer were wounded. Other terrified employees hid or were forced to lie on the ground. After the initial confusion subsided, two Alianzistas decided to take hostages, a journalist who later managed to escape, and a deputy sheriff, whom they let go shortly thereafter. Tijerina and the rest of the Alianzistas fled into the nearby mountains.

Lasting just 90 minutes, the raid unleashed the full force of New Mexican law enforcement, including 450 National Guardsmen, tanks and helicopters, 150 state police officers, dozens of state mounted patrolmen, and even Apache tribal police on horseback. In what was dubbed the "largest manhunt in New Mexican state history," 50 Alianza family members (including children) were rounded up and held in a livestock corral without shelter or drinking water. Tijerina's wife Patsy was arrested as well, all in an attempt to bring him out of hiding. He was finally captured six days later, found hiding in a car on the way to Albuquerque.

For better or for worse, Tijerina and the Alianza would forever be associated with the Tierra Amarilla courthouse raid. It was inspirational to Chicano activists who sought dramatic change, but the event's sensational nature allowed it to be easily manipulated by

## ALL THAT FOR ONE MAN?

Tijerina's detractors. In fact, the aggressive government response to the raid was spurred in part by outlandish rumors that Communist Cuban guerrillas were at the helm and that urban Alianza cells were ready to rise up in revolt. The courthouse raid brought Tijerina national attention, prompting comparisons with the African American civil rights leader Stokely Carmichael and the Cuban revolutionary Che Guevara, both of whom had called for militant action in the fight for justice. In any event, what was once a regional issue focused on land grants was now front-page news across the country, and the more nationalistic rhetoric that ensued added another dimension to the rapidly growing Chicano Movement. No longer were Tijerina's supporters content with centuries-old claims in legal documents; many were calling for the establishment of a Chicano homeland.

Serving as his own defense, Tijerina was acquitted of charges

# TIJERINA OFTEN TOLD

THE FABLE OF THE CRICKET DEFEATING THE LION: 'IF THAT CRICKET GETS IN THE EAR OF THE LION AND SCRATCHES INSIDE, THERE IS NOTHING THE LION CAN DO...THERE IS NO WAY THE LION CAN USE HIS CLAWS AND JAWS TO DESTROY THE CRICKET.'

stemming from the courthouse raid. He continued to organize the Alianza, most notably in an October 1967 conference that attracted civil rights activists from around the country. Among them were Black Power militants, New Left radicals, Native American activists, and almost a "who's who" of future Chicano activists. In spring 1968, Martin Luther King, Jr., shortly before his assassination, asked Tijerina to represent Mexican Americans in the Poor People's Campaign, a Washington D.C., march calling for economic justice.

Thus, in short time, Tijerina became one of the Chicano Movement's most recognizable leaders. But the New Mexican state authorities didn't give up so easily. Tijerina eventually faced charges for the Echo Amphitheater takeover, the courthouse raid, and an incident involving his wife, Patsy, in which a National Forest sign was burned. In 1969, he was convicted and served two years in federal prison. The only Chicano Movement leader of his stature to serve significant prison time, Tijerina, upon his release, would find the Alianza movement in shambles and his influence greatly diminished.

## EL GRITO DEL NORTE AND BETITA MARTÍNEZ

*El Grito del Norte* was another newspaper that was established to support La Alianza's efforts but that soon evolved into one of the Chicano Movement's most important publications. *El Grito* addressed issues beyond the land grant movement, speaking out against the war in Vietnam, defending workers' rights and Latino political prisoners, and connecting the land struggle in New Mexico to land struggles throughout the world. Founded in 1968 by Elizabeth "Betita" Martínez and movement attorney Beverly Axelrod, *El Grito* had a staff of columnists, writers, artists, and photographers made up largely of women. In contrast to Alianza, whose leadership was primarily male, the paper presented a strong feminist stance.

Betita Martínez had participated in the southern civil rights movement and was a member of the Student Nonviolent Coordinating Committee (SNCC), an influential student group that organized sit-ins and the famous Freedom Rides to register voters. In addition to serving as founder and managing editor of *El Grito*, Martínez went on to publish *450 Years of Chicano History in Pictures* (later *500 Years of Chicano History in Pictures*) and a companion volume titled *500 Years of Chicana Women's History*. When *El Grito* ceased publication in 1973, Martínez co-founded and directed the Chicano Communications Center, a community-based educational project in Albuquerque, New Mexico.

Martínez's staunch feminism, internationalist perspective, and wealth of experience as an editor, writer, and activist in the 1960s and '70s made her a role model for Chicana activism.

# RODOLFO "CORKY" GONZALEZ AND THE CRUSADE FOR JUSTICE

As the Chicano Movement gained momentum in the late 1960s, Rodolfo "Corky" Gonzales and his Denver, Colorado-based community organization, the Crusade for Justice, emerged to articulate a larger vision. Although Chávez and the farmworkers' struggle and Tijerina's land grant efforts inspired Mexican Americans across the country, those leaders were cautious about their association with a broader nationalist movement typified by ethnic pride. The language and actions of both their campaigns certainly alluded to a broader Mexican American plight, but both focused on specific, concrete goals (labor concessions and land grants). In contrast, Corky Gonzales's calls for community self-determination hinted at a more ambitious and revolutionary vision. Significantly, his goals were couched in the rhetoric of a new "Chicano" identity, most notably in his 1967 epic poem *Yo Soy Joaquín/I am Joaquín*, which spoke to the history of oppression and survival shared by Mexican Americans everywhere.

Gonzales and the Crusade for Justice played an important part in the 1968 Poor People's Campaign in Washington D.C., where they, along with Tijerina, argued for more inclusion of the Mexican American community in the march's goals. A year later, the Crusade for Justice would organize one the most influential gatherings of the Chicano Movement—the 1969 Chicano Youth and Liberation Conference in Denver, Colorado; that meeting resulted in *El Plan Espiritual de Aztlán*, a founding document of Chicano nationalism. Lastly, and perhaps most importantly, Gonzales and the Crusade for Justice gave voice to young Chicanos, in particular those from urban barrios, which signaled a dramatic shift in the focus and energy of the Movement.

# RODOLFO "CORKY" GONZALES

Born on June 18, 1928, Corky Gonzales was only slightly younger than Tijerina and Chávez, yet his appeal was mainly with Mexican American youth. Much of that had to do with the details of his personal transformation. As a member of the Mexican-American Generation, Gonzalez began with the belief that assimilation was the only path to acceptance in American society. A former professional boxer of significant acclaim, he owned a neighborhood tavern called Corky's

I BLEED AS THE VICIOUS GLOVES OF HUNGER CUT MY FACE AND EYES, AS I FIGHT MY WAY FROM STINKING BARRIOS TO THE GLAMOUR OF THE RING AND LIGHTS OF FAME OR MUTILATED SORROW.

— CORKY GONZALES

CORKY GONZALES DENVER, COLORADO
63 WINS, 11 LOSSES

Corner and a bail bonds business. Also active in Democratic Party politics, he ran a highly successful Viva Kennedy! Club in 1960— part of a national campaign effort to bring Mexican Americans to the polls—and became known in political circles for carrying great weight with Denver's Mexican American community. As a result, he was appointed to positions of leadership in various government programs, including Denver's War on Poverty program, President Lyndon B. Johnson's sweeping antipoverty initiative, and the city's Neighborhood Youth Corps. By all accounts, he was headed for elective office.

It was in those leadership roles, however, that Gonzales began to see holes in the promise of assimilation and electoral politics as a

AND SO LITTLE
EMILIANO DECIDED
THAT THE LAND
SHOULD BELONG TO
THOSE WHO
WORKED IT.

ESCUELA TLATELOLCO

vehicle for change. He realized that the Democratic Party was happy to have Mexican American voters but fielded few Mexican American candidates and rarely catered to the community's interests. In his work as a bail bondsman, he saw firsthand the brutality and mistreatment of Mexican Americans at the hands of law enforcement, including the use of lethal force. In response, he and other community leaders in 1963 formed Los Voluntarios (The Volunteers) to advocate on behalf of Mexican Americans. In the next two years, as confrontations escalated with city officials, only to be met with indifference, Gonzales's disillusionment with mainstream politics increased.

In 1966, afterv resigning his membership in the Democratic Party and his positions with government antipoverty programs, he established one of the first Mexican American civil rights organizations, called the Crusade for Justice. Adopting many of the same goals as the federal War on Poverty, but pursuing them without government support, the Crusade for Justice forged an ethos of self-determination and community control. That spirit would eventually give rise to a host of initiatives, including a school (Escuela Tlatelolco), job training programs, athletic leagues, an art gallery, a community center, a newspaper called *El Gallo*, and a number of social and legal services. In addition to fostering a stronger sense of ethnic pride, Gonzales and the Crusade for Justice espoused a platform of cultural nationalism—both pride in being of Mexican origin and rejection of Anglo cultural and economic domination. An activist platform, it also called for a new, more politicized ethnic identity. To articulate this new way of thinking, Gonzales wrote *Yo Soy Joaquín/I am Joaquín* in 1967. Distributed and recited at rallies, community meetings, and college campuses, it became a foundational work of Chicano Movement literature.

## I AM JOAQUÍN

The epic poem *I am Joaquín* reads like an essay in verse that traces the history of Mexican Americans dating back to the Spanish conquest of Mesoamerica. It references proud indigenous civilizations, the brutality of Spanish and American colonialism, the heroes of Mexican Independence and the Mexican Revolution, as well as the futility of Mexican Americans seeking acceptance in Anglo society that uses them for their labor but treats them with disdain. For many Mexican Americans who had never been exposed to their history in school, let alone read a book that placed them at the center of the narrative, *I am Joaquín* was by turns a stunning history lesson, a rousing battle cry, and a powerful organizing tool. Luis Valdez and Teatro Campesino later turned the poem into a film that further exposed audiences to imagery that many had never seen before: Mesoamerican sculptures; murals by Diego Rivera, David

HAVE YOU SEEN THIS FILM BEFORE?

SIX TIMES.

Alfaro Siqueiros, and José Clemente Orozco depicting the history of Mexico; and historical photographs depicting poverty and violence but also proud perseverance. Whether read, performed aloud, or viewed on film, *I am Joaquín* was instrumental in creating a sense of what it meant to be Chicano, a label used with ever greater frequency among Mexican Americans involved in the Movement.

The declaration "I am Joaquín" is not intended to indicate a single narrator's story, but rather the collective experience of a people. The poem represents a search for identity in a world that has sought to crush the spirit and soul of Mexican Americans. Joaquín is a symbol and personification of his people.

*I am Joaquín, lost in a world of confusion,*
*caught up in the whirl of a gringo society,*
*confused by the rules, scorned by attitudes,*
*suppressed by manipulation, and destroyed by*
    *modern society.*

The poem seeks to counteract that destruction by discovering or revealing the true, proud history inherited by Mexican Americans. This includes the concept that Mexican Americans, as mestizos, were both conquerors and conquered, the "sword and flame of Cortés the despot" as well as the "the eagle and serpent of the Aztec civilization." And it reaffirms the fact that Mexican American history was rooted in North America before the arrival of European colonists and the European immigrants who became part of the Anglo society that rejected them.

The poem also details a history of exploitation, violence, and discrimination. ("My back of Indian slavery was stripped of crimson/ from the whips of masters"; "My hands calloused from the hoe/I have made the Anglo rich"). But beyond that it celebrates the resilience of a culture and community that has persevered.

*I am the masses of my people and*
*I refuse to be absorbed.*
*I am Joaquín.*
*The odds are great.*
*But my spirit is strong.*

Throughout, Joaquín identifies himself with heroes of Mexican and Mexican American history who stood up to oppression. He ends with a call to defy society's pressures to assimilate or disappear: "I SHALL ENDURE/I WILL ENDURE."

Articulating an identity rooted in resistance, *I am Joaquín* appealed to young Mexican Americans increasingly politicized by the events taking place throughout the country. The poem and the subsequent film synthesized complex ideas and elicited strong emotion. As Chicanos searched for a way to describe who they were and what they wanted, *I am Joaquín* gave them the language to do so and instilled them with pride. It also pointed to the importance that the arts could have in building cultural and political consciousness.

# CHICANO YOUTH AND LIBERATION CONFERENCE

The 1968 Poor People's Campaign in Washington, D.C., brought Corky Gonzales and the Crusade for Justice national visibility and identified Gonzales as one of the key leaders of the Chicano Movement. Along with Tijerina, Gonzales argued for Mexican Americans to have more input in the campaign's efforts, which were largely dominated by African Americans. Despite significant discord, the campaign represented the first time that broad-based initiatives were introduced jointly by Mexican Americans, African Americans, and Native Americans to promote economic justice and land rights. Led by Gonzales, Mexican American participants also produced a declaration called *El Plan del Barrio,* which outlined measures to provide separate public housing for Mexican Americans, bilingual education, community-owned businesses, and restitution of community land grants.

Upon their return from Washington, the Crusade for Justice bought an old church in downtown Denver and established it as their headquarters. From there they sought to build upon their ideas of self-determination, or community control. And so they began planning a conference to bring together a network of Chicano activist organizations from around the country.

The philosophy of Chicano nationalism as espoused by Corky Gonzales and the Crusade for Justice was central to the planning and tone of the event. Spanning five days in March 1969, the Chicano Youth and Liberation Conference attracted more than a thousand youth, mainly from Texas, the Southwest, California, the Pacific Northwest, and the Great Lakes region. From New York and Chicago came a few members of the Puerto Rican Young Lords, a community self-defense group modeled after the Black Panthers. Many of the conference attendees were from newly formed Mexican American student organizations that had been popping up on college campuses. In addition to students, there were labor leaders, urban political groups, community activists, as well as *vatos locos* (street youth)

and *pintos* (ex-convicts). In fact, the anti-establishment tone of the conference placed special emphasis on the vatos locos, their dress, and their fraternal code; many of their crimes were viewed as models of societal rejection.

Conference participants attended seminars and panels on organizing, activism, and self-defense as well as Chicano culture and gender issues. They painted, read poetry, debated, and networked with other activists from different parts of the country. In the process, they learned what commonalities they shared, as well as each other's regional differences.

With nationalist ideology driving the discussion, participants stressed unity among all Mexican Americans regardless of region or social class. Everyone would be united in the struggle against oppression, exploitation, and racism. As Third World countries in Asia, Africa, and Latin America were fighting against colonialism and the dominance of European and American imperialism, Chicanos began to see their struggle in the same light: they too had been colonized by mainstream American society, stripped of their culture, and taught to be ashamed of who they were and where they came from.

And with that shared understanding came a shared desire to be liberated. Mexican Americans needed to be instilled with pride in their ethnicity and culture; they needed to reject the dominant values of American society, including capitalism and white Anglo-Saxon

Protestant culture. Inherent in this rejection or "liberation" was a vague sense of separatism, the notion that Chicano communities needed complete autonomy in order to thrive.

Conference participants would be at the helm of spreading these ideas. In order to help facilitate this mobilization, they developed a series of resolutions comprising *El Plan Espiritual de Aztlán*, a political manifesto and a guide for future Chicano activism.

# EL PLAN ESPIRITUAL DE AZTLÁN

The preamble to *El Plan Espiritual de Aztlán* (The Spiritual Plan of Aztlán) clearly articulates several emerging ideas of the Chicano Movement. First, the rise of Chicano consciousness as a twofold experience—the awareness of a rich history, and the rejection of Anglo society and values: "In the spirit of a new people that is conscious not only of its proud historical heritage but also of the brutal 'gringo' invasion of our territories." Second, that central to this emerging consciousness was a belief in a Chicano homeland: "We, the Chicano inhabitants and civilizers of the northern land of Aztlán from whence came our forefathers, reclaiming the land of their birth and consecrating the determination of our people of the sun." And third, that tying the American Southwest to Aztlán, the mythical homeland of the Aztecs, was a way to achieve unity among Mexican Americans everywhere.

## Aztlán

According to Aztec legend, their ancestors had left Aztlán after receiving a prophecy to migrate south to an area called Anáhuac, where they built the great city of Tenochtitlán (near what is now Mexico City). Aztlán was located north of what we now know as Mexico, more or less in the American Southwest. Thus, as introduced by the radical Chicano poet Alurista, the modern concept of Aztlán recognized Chicano identity as rooted in Native American tradition, myth, and legend. To do so was as important politically as it was psychologically or spiritually; the Chicano Movement was young, but the history of Chicanos in the Southwest was not. As the Chicano author Rudolfo Anaya wrote,

WE KNEW WE COULD TURN TO THE TREATY OF GUADALUPE HIDALGO, A HISTORICAL TREATY BETWEEN NATIONS, TO DEFINE OURSELVES AS MEXICANS WITH CERTAIN RIGHTS WITHIN THE BORDERS OF THE UNITED STATES, BUT THAT POLITICAL DEFINITION HAD

WELCOME TO AZTLÁN!

WITH YOUR GUIDE, THE POET ALURISTA

NEVER BEEN ENOUGH. A GROUP DEFINES ITSELF NOT ONLY POLITICALLY, BUT ALSO BY ITS CHARACTER, THAT IS, ITS SOUL.

Aztlán provided that soul, connecting Chicanos to thousands of years of history in the Americas. For fledgling Chicano writers and artists like Alurista, Anaya, and Luis Valdez, Aztlán and its accompanying legends became a trove of imagery and thought.

## THE PROGRAM: ORGANIZATIONAL GOALS AND ACTIONS

*El Plan Espiritual de Aztlán* included seven organizational goals and six plans of action. Nationalism was the unifying force, defined both by pride in culture and history and by the quest for self-determination, an independent and self-reliant Mexican American community. The *Plan's* first goal promoted unity among Mexican Americans regardless of geography or social class: "all should be committed to the liberation of La Raza." Other goals included autonomous institutions and community control over the economy, education, and self-defense. In regard to the economy, the goal was to "drive the exploiter out of our communities" and set up a system that rejected materialism and embraced humanistic values of cooperation and distribution of wealth and resources. Similarly in education, the document advocated community control and a curriculum relevant to Chicanos.

The *Plan Espiritual* called on official institutions to do more than offer "handouts," but to serve the Mexican American community based on restitution for past injustices. It called on the Chicano people to be the first line of defense against exploiters and outside forces seeking to damage the community. And it called on artists and cultural workers to create work that educated and united the Chicano community in a "revolutionary culture." Lastly, the

A GLOSSARY OF SORTS

document dismissed the two-party political system as unable to meet the needs of Mexican Americans; the goal would be to organize politically: "Where we are a majority, we will control; where we are a minority, we will represent a pressure group."

The plans of action began with distribution of *El Plan Espiritual de Aztlán* to "every place of human existence" and the enactment of organizational goals, including a nationwide walkout of all Chicano students to demand educational reform. They also called for the

creation of an independent political party, a hint of the political mobilization soon to come.

Perhaps just as significant was what didn't find its way into the final *Plan Espiritual:* a resolution pertaining to gender equality. A group of Chicana feminists had organized a workshop to draft a resolution of their own, but resistance was strong; a number of Chicanas worried that a feminist resolution would be too divisive. With conference leaders calling for unity behind a nationalist ideology, it was difficult for many women to raise the issues of patriarchy, sexism, and machismo. Further complicating the situation was a belief that feminism was a "white women's issue." Chicanas who raised it were often called *vendidas,* or sellouts. Indicative of this attitude, and the general chauvinism prevalent at the time, Gonzales himself stated in a 1970 speech,

> I RECOGNIZE TOO MUCH OF AN INFLUENCE OF WHITE EUROPEAN THINKING IN THE DISCUSSION. I HOPE THAT OUR CHICANA SISTERS CAN UNDERSTAND THAT THEY CAN BE FRONTRUNNERS IN THE REVOLUTION, THEY CAN BE IN THE LEADERSHIP OF ANY SOCIAL MOVEMENT, BUT I PRAY TO GOD THAT THEY DO NOT LOSE THEIR CHICANISMA OR THEIR WOMANHOOD AND BECOME A FRIGID GRINGA. SO I'M FOR EQUALITY, BUT STILL WANT TO SEE SOME SEX IN OUR WOMEN.

Chicanas at the conference finally gave in. When delegates met to vote on the resolutions to be included in the *Plan,* the Chicana Caucus reported that, "It was the consensus of the group that the Chicana does not want to be liberated." Many Chicanas were deeply disappointed and left the conference dedicated to ensuring that their voices, already silenced by Anglo society, would not also be squashed by their own.

# ENRIQUETA VASQUEZ

Enriqueta Vasquez was an activist and writer who worked closely with both the Crusade for Justice in Colorado and the Alianza in New Mexico. She first met Corky Gonzales when they spearheaded the War on Poverty programs together in Denver. Vasquez deeply admired Gonzales and his leadership, but she also found herself ambivalent about how to reconcile cultural nationalism and the patriarchal tendencies it reinforced, i.e., the man as head of the family, the leader. Later, Vasquez and her husband, the artist Bill Longley, moved to northern New Mexico to establish a Crusade for Justice center that would link its efforts to Tijerina and the Alianza. She became well known as a columnist for *El Grito del Norte*, posing some of the hardest questions facing Chicano activists, in particular the role of Chicana feminism in the movement.

*El Plan Espiritual de Aztlán* was a radical document. To read it today is to get a glimpse into the mindset of Chicano youth hungry for revolutionary change. Still, the concept of Chicano nationalism remained ambiguous in the overall Movement. Some viewed it as a separatist agenda, a literal call for a Chicano homeland or sovereign state to be established separate from the Anglo-dominated United States. More commonly it was viewed something like the concept of Aztlán—a kind of spiritual reclamation, the desire for a homeland where Chicanos could achieve self-determination and exert control over their communities, their education, and the political process. For many, it was simply a call for agency rather than passivity, pride rather than shame, hopefulness rather than helplessness.

As young activists left the Denver Youth Conference armed with clear organization goals and plans of action, they were bent on spreading the impact across the country. And they were largely successful. The conference far exceeded the Crusade for Justice's expectations and solidified Corky Gonzales's cultural nationalist framework for the Chicano Movement. César Chávez and Reies López Tijerina had been instrumental in bringing the plight of Mexican Americans into the national spotlight and the larger civil rights struggle. But their efforts remained focused on specific issues—labor and land rights—that pertained to rural communities, whereas the majority of Mexican Americans now lived in cities. Gonzales and the Crusade for Justice pushed the movement into the realm of urban youth and onto high school and college campuses. From there, a new generation of ethnically conscious, politically energized Mexican Americans—now calling themselves Chicanos—escalated the demands and dreams of the Movement.

# 4

## ESCALATION: YOUTH MOBILIZATION, MILITANCY, AND CONFLICT

YOUTH CARRY THE
MOVEMENT FORWARD

While the emergence of the Chicano Movement certainly owed much to individual leaders and organizations, it's important to know that this was not a movement of a select few but of many—and most of them were young people. César Chávez, Dolores Huerta, Reies López Tijerina, and Corky Gonzales certainly inspired Mexican Americans across the country, giving visibility to the community's struggles against poverty, discrimination, and racism, and to its general marginalization in Anglo society. But what made the Chicano Movement a movement was what young Mexican Americans did with that inspiration. Influenced by a multitude of factors—experience working with federal antipoverty programs, exposure to the African American civil rights struggle, protests against the Vietnam War, and awareness of Third World anticolonial and liberation struggles (such as the Cuban Revolution)—young Mexican Americans began to mobilize and form their own organizations on college campuses across the Southwest.

In 1964, Armando Valdez organized the Student Initiative (SI) at San José State College, the first student organization to focus on the needs of Mexican Americans. Two years later, the Mexican American Youth Organization (MAYO) was established at St. Mary's College in San Antonio, Texas, and the Mexican American Student Organization (MASO) was founded at the University of Texas at Austin. Chapters of United Mexican American Studies (UMAS) were formed on numerous campuses in Los Angeles, and the Mexican American Student Association (MASA) was launched at East Los Angeles Community College. In Northern California, the Student Initiative at San José State College changed its name to the Mexican American Student Confederation (MASC), and subsequent chapters were established at other area colleges and universities, including the University of California, Berkeley, in 1968.

Although organizations such as these continued to proliferate, their goals were in no way uniform. All of them emerged out of a need to give Mexican American students a voice. Far from radical, most of the organizations believed, like the Mexican-American Generation before them, that education was the key to success. They worked for recruitment and retention, sought out Mexican American professionals to fund scholarships, and organized around electoral politics. But as the 1960s civil rights struggle gave way to more militant mass protests (epitomized by the Black Power movement) and as the likes of Tijerina and Gonzales espoused a more confrontational philosophy, some Chicano youth groups began to eschew middle-of-the-road politics and activism.

At first, student activists played a supportive role. They invited Chávez, Tijerina, and Gonzales to speak on their campuses, they organized caravans to bring food to the striking farmworkers in Delano, and they helped provide much-needed manpower at supermarket picket lines to support the grape boycott. As more students began to identify with *Chicanismo*—the Chicano worldview and ideology—and as cultural nationalism engendered a more critical view of traditional "Mexican American" identity, they began to coalesce around issues that impacted them directly as students and as urban youth, such as the failures of the educational system, police brutality, and the war in Vietnam. In 1968, with student demonstrations exploding around the world, many Chicano students began to believe that they were not just supporters of the Movement but a driving force.

## STUDENT WALKOUTS AND THE BROWN BERETS

On the morning of March 3, 1968, students at Lincoln High School in East Los Angeles walked out of their classes. Later in the day, some 10,000 Chicano students from area high schools joined them, crippling the largest school district in the country and bringing the

full weight of law enforcement against them. The students carried signs that read "Chicano Power" and "*Viva la Revolución*" (Long Live the Revolution), but their demands were hardly radical. Led by Sal Castro, a Lincoln High School teacher, they called for the elimination of discriminatory school policies and racist teachers; they sought a curriculum that addressed Mexican American history and culture; and they wanted more Mexican American faculty members and administrators. With high school dropout rates near 50%, students were calling out a school system that had failed them, rather than that they had failed.

College students from nearby universities, including members of UMAS, joined the striking students, handing out picket signs and assisting organizers with their list of demands. The Brown Berets, a nascent Chicano self-defense organization, showed up in case

police tried to intimidate the students. In all likelihood, their presence only increased police aggression. With the media spotlight on East Los Angeles, law-enforcement officers attempted to disperse students at Roosevelt High School, who claimed their legal right to demonstrate. The situation quickly escalated into outright violence, as officers of the LAPD were captured on film brutally beating student demonstrators. Parents and community members, many of whom had been skeptical of the students' tactics, were swayed to their side. The police response was clearly incommensurate and incompatible with student demands for better treatment and a more equitable system.

The walkouts, or "blowouts" as they were called, led to the formation of the Educational Issues Coordinating Committee (EICC), composed of parents, community members, high school students, and members of UMAS. Together with the strikers, the EICC pressured the board of education to hold a special session to hear student demands. There were 36 demands in all, ranging from bilingual education and better facilities to community control of the schools. On March 28, some 1,200 people attended a community meeting held at Lincoln High, where board members listened to student and parent grievances and claimed to be sympathetic, but denied any prejudice in the allocation of funding and claimed to have insufficient resources for the proposed changes. Two weeks later, the EICC, frustrated at the lack of response or concrete action on the part of officials, led a group of 800 protestors to occupy school board offices.

SO WHILE THE SCHOOL BOARD IS CERTAINLY SYMPATHETIC TO YOUR GRIEVANCES, PLEASE UNDERSTAND THAT IT'S IN OUR BEST INTEREST TO DO NOTHING.

## EAST L.A. 13

Even though school board members had gone on record opposing discipline for the participants in the strike, law enforcement on June 2 arrested 13 organizers of the walkouts. Among them were student activists from UMAS, members of the Brown Berets, antipoverty workers, publishers of a local Chicano newspaper, and Lincoln High School teacher Sal Castro. They were all labeled "outside agitators"

CLEAR—CUT CASE OF CONSPIRACY TO DISTURB THE PEACE!

EXCLUSIVE! LA RAZA NEWSPAPER □ VOICE OF THE CHICANO BARRIO

PUBLISHERS OF LA RAZA ARRESTED

and charged with conspiracy to disturb the peace. Although disturbing the peace was a misdemeanor, conspiracy made it a felony and raised the possibility of time in prison. Sal Castro was immediately barred from teaching.

The criminal indictment of the East L.A. 13, or ELA13, triggered protests against the Los Angeles Police Department and demonstrations in support of the arrestees. The Chicano Legal Defense Fund and Attorneys for Civil Liberties raised funds for legal expenses, and Chicano Movement lawyer Oscar Zeta Acosta defended the activists. After a series of dramatic sit-ins and protests, the school board reinstated Sal Castro and all charges against the ELA13 were eventually dismissed. With attention focused primarily on the legal case, student activism in the schools subsided.

The East L.A. blowouts brought national attention to the failure of the educational system to serve Mexican American youth. It was also the first mass Mexican American protest against racism. Whereas the farmworkers' strike and the land grant movement had focused on issues that related to injustice and mistreatment of Mexican Americans, the striking students directly spelled out the effects of racism and discrimination. And though Sal Castro played a key role at the outset, the strike leadership was composed almost entirely of students, both male and female. The walkouts demonstrated to students in other parts of the country that they, too, could

SAL CASTRO IS FIRED

demand change, and the next two years brought strikes throughout the Southwest, including in Denver, and in Crystal City, Texas.

In addition, despite the students' reform-minded demands, the aggressive response by law enforcement and the lengths to which the schools, the police, and the courts were willing to go to suppress their constitutional rights, increasingly radicalized Chicano youth and the Movement as a whole. The Mexican American community had long felt that they were struggling against a system that sought to repress them. The response to the blowouts gave them tangible evidence that not only was this case, but that democratic pleas to authority were futile. That sentiment gave rise to the so-called Brown Power movement, reflected above all in the emergence of the Brown Berets.

## THE BROWN BERETS

Ironically, the blowouts and the Brown Berets, the most militant group of the Chicano Movement, originated at a high school leadership camp in Malibu, California. Sponsored by the Los Angeles County Commission on Human Relations, the annual Mexican-American Youth Leadership Conference brought together high-achieving Mexican American students with the hope that they would go on to leadership positions and have a positive impact in their communities. Held at Camp Hess Kramer, the conference had students staying in cabins with counselors and workshop leaders. While its mission was ostensibly assimilationist, the event had the opposite effect: high-school age Mexican Americans were exposed to more politicized college students, who in turn shared their progressive ideas. Bright-eyed youth entered the camp focused on leadership activities and left talking about César Chávez and the farmworkers' struggle.

The Young Citizens for Community Action (YCCA) emerged out

HOW 'BOUT WHEN WE GET BACK FROM CAMP WE ORGANIZE A MILITANT BROWN POWER ORGANIZATION?

CAMP HESS KRAMER   MALIBU, CALIFORNIA

of Camp Hess Kramer. Founded in May 1966 by future blowout leaders—among them Vickie Castro, David Sánchez, Moctesuma Esparza, Ralph Ramírez, Rachel Ochoa, George Licon, and John Ortiz—the YCCA began with a belief in conventional politics. Participants created surveys to address students' needs, met with education officials, and worked to elect Julian Nava as the first Mexican American school board member. As the students became more politicized, however, they changed the name of the organization to the Young Chicanos for Community Action. In October 1967, with the help of a supportive priest, Father John B. Luce, the YCCA opened a coffeehouse in East Los Angeles called La Piranya. With the coffeehouse serving as its main office, the organization began hosting prominent leaders of the Chicano Movement, such as Chávez, Reies López Tijerina, and Corky Gonzales, as well as leaders from the Black Power movement, including Stokely Carmichael and Hubert "Rap" Brown. La Piranya sponsored a number of other events and gatherings, most of them focused on encouraging young people to attend college. But local law enforcement saw the coffee shop as a den of radical activity. Sheriff deputies frequently harassed patrons, questioning them extensively and performing illegal searches. Upset by this treatment, YCCA members organized a demonstration at the nearby sheriff's station—to little avail.

A BROWN BERET

In late 1967 and early 1968, as members left for college, they spent less time with the group; among them were two of the female founders, Rachel Ochoa and the YCCA's first president, Vickie Castro. David Sánchez assumed leadership of the organization, and as police harassment continued, the group became notably more militant in its approach. Members took to wearing military khakis and a brown beret adorned with a patch; on it appeared the words "La Causa," over a yellow pentagon, two bayoneted rifles, and a cross. Soon they were calling themselves the Brown Berets. The high school blowouts in March 1968 gave the group wide visibility as a community self-defense organization similar to the Black Panthers. Most of the members were young adults who saw it as their duty to protect the younger demonstrators from the police.

During the summer following the blowouts, the Brown Berets developed a "Ten Point Program" to articulate their goals; these, too, were modeled after the Black Panthers. The ten points included many of the demands made by student demonstrators, including bilingual education and a curriculum relevant to Mexican Americans. Another was police accountability, including the hiring of officers who spoke Spanish and were sensitive to the community's needs. Other goals included economic justice, fair housing, the right to vote regardless of the ability to speak English, a jury of peers, and the right to bear arms to defend their communities. Essentially, the Brown Berets were asking for the Mexican American community's basic rights as guaranteed under the U.S. Constitution. Their motto "to serve, to observe, and to protect," proclaimed that the Brown Berets would be present and watchful to ensure that government agencies, especially law enforcement, respected these rights. Early members did include women, though they soon grew disenchanted by their exclusion and subordination within the organization. They eventually split off and formed Las Adelitas de Aztlán, which, though short-lived, encouraged other women who found their voices suppressed within the Movement.

Ultimately, the Brown Berets' paramilitary appearance was more symbolic than anything else, used to emphasize an ethos of self-discipline and self-respect. The group stressed community unity and organizational discipline. As leader David Sánchez wrote at the time, "Because your people, the land, and the enemy are watching you, you must look good, act right, and move with the precision of a clock." Brown Berets were expected to hold a high standard of personal conduct, which included dressing well, being fair and courteous

THE BROWN BERETS

to others, and serving as an example for the community. Although some members certainly sought more revolutionary action, the Brown Beret's espousal of violence—protection of the community by "any means necessary"—was a matter of rhetoric rather than of action. This didn't mean there was no violence, or that the Brown Berets were ineffective as a community self-defense organization. The Brown Berets inspired countless chapters throughout the country—in such places as Kansas City, Missouri; Seattle, Washington; and Minnesota—comprising thousands of members. They also inspired similar organizations, such as the Black Berets and Los Comancheros in New Mexico. Finally, the Brown Berets created a free medical clinic in East Los Angeles, and were instrumental in the Chicano antiwar effort and helping to plan the seminal Chicano Moratorium of 1969 and 1970.

## CHE GUEVARA

The Argentinean freedom fighter Ernesto "Che" Guevara, who fought in the Cuban Revolution and the Congo before his death in Bolivia after a failed military campaign in 1967, became an iconic figure and ubiquitous image in the Chicano Movement.

ARE WE TRYING TO LOOK LIKE SOMEONE IN PARTICULAR? NO, WHY DO YOU ASK?

His face was emblazoned on countless pamphlets, newspapers, posters, murals, and banners. Those who understood the Chicano Movement as a struggle against colonialism and imperialism viewed Che as a defender of the poor who was willing to rise up in arms against oppression and tyranny. In a famous mural at Stanford University titled *The Chicano Last Supper*, Chicano artist José Antonio Burciaga replaced Jesus with Che Guevara at the center of the table.

# THE CHICANO MORATORIUM

By the late 1960s, the anti-Vietnam War movement had grown to hundreds of thousand strong, with countless demonstrations and university campus strikes across the country. Public support for U.S. involvement waned dramatically as the war dragged on with no end in sight and as the number of casualties rose. The Mexican American community was slow to turn against the war, however, in part because of a proud history of serving in the U.S. military; this had long been viewed as a way to prove one's patriotism and contribution to society at large. Organizations such as the American GI Forum lobbied on behalf of Mexican American veterans, arguing that their service entitled them to respect and equal treatment. But as more and more Mexican Americans returned home in body bags and in disproportionate numbers—Mexican Americans represented more than 20% of casualties in the Southwest but only 10% of the population—it became harder to support the war effort. What's more, as the Chicano Movement gave visibility to the mistreatment faced by the Mexican American community, many began to question why young Chicanos were fighting poor brown people in Vietnam when the real struggle was in the barrios at home.

Chicanos began to refuse induction into the armed forces; among them were such prominent activists as Salomón Baldenegro of Tucson, Arizona; Ernesto Vigil of Denver's Crusade for Justice; and Rosalio Muñoz, a former student body president at University of California, Los Angeles. On September 16, 1969, Muñoz attempted

to bring attention to his draft refusal by holding a protest at the local induction center. In a speech delivered that day, he declared his independence from the Selective Service: "I accuse the draft, the entire social, political, and economic system of the United States of America of creating a funnel which shoots Mexican youth into Vietnam to be killed and to kill innocent men, women, and children." Traveling around the Southwest speaking to other activists about the draft, Muñoz became convinced that what was needed was a national Chicano peace protest.

Meanwhile, earlier that year, the Brown Berets had returned from the Denver Chicano Youth and Liberation Conference, where they had discussed the war's negative impact. Corky Gonzales and the Crusade for Justice had long voiced opposition to the war based on the disproportionate toll it took on poor communities. Thus, many youth left the conference convinced that they needed to raise awareness back home. On December 19, 1969, the Brown Berets held the first Chicano Moratorium Committee (CMC) rally at Obregon Park in East L.A. The turnout of nearly 2,000 people surprised organizers, who immediately began planning another one. They also asked Muñoz to be a co-chairman of the planning committee.

On February 28, 1970, the CMC organized another rally at nearby Salazar Park, this one attended by 5,000 people. The event brought significant attention to the CMC, which decided to build on the momentum and organize yet another, even larger moratorium on August 29. The CMC was renamed the National Chicano Moratorium Committee (NCMC), and with the financial support of the Southwest Council of La Raza, Muñoz began organizing full time for the event. At the Second Annual Chicano Youth Conference that

March in Denver, Muñoz garnered the support of Corky Gonzales and fellow draft resister Ernesto Vigil. In the months leading up to the national moratorium, attendees sponsored hundreds of antiwar demonstrations throughout the Southwest.

Although everyone was united against the war, not all the organizers agreed politically. The more radical activists opposed the war for anti-colonialist or anti-imperialist reasons; many of them even sided with the Viet Cong and their leader Ho Chi Minh, viewing him as a freedom fighter in the same vein as Che Guevara. Others saw the war and its draft policy—which left Chicanos few opportunities for deferment—as a genocidal conspiracy against minorities who were dying in inordinate numbers while their communities languished at home. The more moderate activists, uncomfortable with these more controversial reasons, simply couldn't accept the countless flag-draped coffins returning home from a war being fought for reasons they didn't understand. Some of these political differences played out in organizing the moratorium, as almost 150 people ended up on the steering committee.

Despite the division among organizers, thousands of activists arrived from all over the United States on August 29, 1970, to join the local Mexican American community march three miles down Whittier Boulevard toward Laguna Park, where the main rally was to be held. The organizing committee had recruited hundreds of monitor-volunteers to preserve the peace and quell any disturbances. They were joined by hundreds of stone-faced police officers and sheriff deputies, who erected barricades along the parade route and by all accounts were prepared for a riot. In the largest mass protest in Mexican American history, indeed the largest antiwar effort by any American minority group, between 20,000 and 30,000 people took part in the Chicano Moratorium. Most of the demonstrators were young, but there were also many families with children. The mood was festive as musicians and performers entertained the crowd.

Despite the heavy police presence, none of the marchers expected the violence that ensued.

Responding to a disturbance at a nearby liquor store where local youth stole soft drinks and beer, police found their excuse to break up the demonstration. As Rosalio Muñoz was about to speak, squad cars descended upon the park and police officers in full riot gear began forcing participants to leave. Some of the demonstrators, angry at the mistreatment, hurled objects at the officers. They, in turn, responded with even more aggression, wielding their clubs and moving across the park in military formation. Tear gas canisters were fired at the crowd. Men, women, and children, many of whom hadn't heard the orders to disperse or were simply confused by the unfolding events, were trapped and panicked. Frustrated protestors began to riot and were viciously clubbed by police. Others were caught up in the mayhem and trampled.

By the time the smoke cleared, several hundred demonstrators had been arrested, including Corky Gonzales, one of the slated speakers.

Sixty demonstrators were wounded, and two Chicano youths were killed; one of them was a 15-year-old Brown Beret. Perhaps the most alarming result of the violence was the death of Ruben Salazar, a respected journalist for the *Los Angeles Times* who had become an inadvertent spokesperson for the Chicano Movement. Salazar's death and the brutal police response to a mostly peaceful demonstration was yet another reminder that the quest for Mexican American civil rights was viewed as a dangerous threat to the status quo.

## RUBEN SALAZAR

Ruben Salazar's death at the Chicano Moratorium transformed him into a Chicano martyr. The irony is that Salazar was far from being a militant. In fact, he was a classic example of the Mexican-American Generation, a middle-class striver who did his job quietly and diligently and kept his distance from politics and civil rights. The bulk of his work as a journalist, including stints as a foreign correspondent in Latin America and war correspondent in Vietnam, displayed no overt criticism of the United States or its policies. When he returned to Los Angeles, Salazar began covering the Mexican American community, which included the growing Chicano activism. His articles

THE POLICE ATTEMPT TO INTIMIDATE RUBEN SALAZAR.

straddled the line; he was both sympathetic to the aims of the protestors while at times criticizing their tactics. Perhaps most importantly, Salazar translated the goals of Chicano activists for a skeptical public and, in a way, explained to Chicanos themselves a clear way of articulating their position to the rest of the world. A good example of this is his *Times* column of February 6, 1970, titled, "Who Is a Chicano? And What Is It the Chicanos Want." In a blunt and succinct opening line, he captures the essence of that identity: "A Chicano is a Mexican-American with a non-Anglo image of himself."

Increasingly, Salazar began reporting on police brutality in the Mexican American community, including the shooting of two innocent Mexican nationals. Dissatisfied with the official police reports, he provided his own coverage of the killings, which prompted two policemen to visit Salazar and request that he tone down his reporting. It was stirring up the Mexican American community, they claimed. Undeterred, Salazar wrote a column about their visit; other intimidation tactics soon followed. Both local law enforcement and the Federal Bureau of Investigation opened files on the reporter, suspecting him of radical activity.

After covering the moratorium march and the mayhem that ensued, Salazar and several fellow journalists stopped at the Silver Dollar, a nearby bar, to have a beer before heading off to write their articles. Shortly after they entered, a sheriff deputy who claimed later that he was responding to a report that a gunman was inside, shot a tear gas projectile into the crowded bar. The 10-inch projectile struck Salazar in the head and killed him. His body lay on the floor for three hours before homicide detectives came to investigate. Eyewitnesses and deputies offered conflicting accounts, and details surrounding the killing remained murky.

Because of his public visibility, along with his prior criticism of

ICONIC IMAGE: THE DEATH OF RUBEN SALAZAR AT THE SILVER DOLLAR

police brutality, many couldn't help but think that the Salazar's death was intentional. Despite photo evidence that showed the deputies ordering bystanders back into the bar and then firing indiscriminately into the crowded establishment, an inquest found that Salazar's death was an accident. The officer was not charged.

Salazar was the first mainstream journalist to cover the Chicano community, and his absence was felt immediately after the moratorium. The newspapers that covered the event at all ran stories regurgitating the police reports. According to a brief article in the *New York Times,* for example, "five hundred policemen and Sheriff's deputies tried to break up roaming gangs." Most newspapers ignored it completely. Salazar, having witnessed the events firsthand, and sympathetic to the cause of the tens of thousands of demonstrators, would have told a far different story.

## Aftermath

Ruben Salazar's death and the police violence at the Chicano Moratorium outraged community members and Chicano activists. Often the moratorium is referred to as the pinnacle of the Chicano Movement—tens of thousands of Chicanos, young and old, gathered to demonstrate for their civil rights—but it was also a moment of great tragedy, and in some ways, the beginning of the Movement's decline. Following the moratorium, organizers planned further protests, this time focused on police brutality. But police responded with more violence, and the intimidation worked: attendance at subsequent rallies dwindled. Law enforcement also escalated tactics to infiltrate and undermine the activist groups, including the National Chicano Moratorium Committee and the Brown Berets. Paranoia fueled division in the ranks, and the organizations became less effective as they focused more on internal squabbles and power struggles.

The energy and shared vision that had inspired the burst of

activism from the high school blowouts in 1968 to the Chicano Moratorium in 1970 had taken a serious blow from which it never truly recovered. Despite public resistance and intense political mobilization, few of the Chicano activists' demands had been met. In *Occupied America*, his classic text of Chicano history, Rodolfo Acuña summarized the state of the Movement at this moment:

> AFTER THE SMOKE CLEARED, IN SPITE OF REAL CHANGE FOR MOST NORTH AMERICANS, VERY LITTLE PROGRESS HAD BEEN MADE BY CHICANOS. THE IMPORTANCE OF ACTIVIST, YOUTH, AND GRASS-ROOTS ORGANIZATIONS DECLINED AFTER THIS POINT. THE 1970S RESTORED TO THE MIDDLE CLASS ITS HEGEMONY OVER THE MOVEMENT.

# CATALINA ISLAND "INVASION"

On August 30, 1972, 26 members of the Brown Berets traveled off the coast of California to Catalina Island and claimed the territory on behalf of all Chicanos. Reminiscent of Tijerina and the Alianza's takeover of Kit Carson National Forest, the occupiers argued that, under the 1848 Treaty of Guadalupe Hidalgo, all coastal lands were still Mexican property. The occupation lasted 24 days and ended when the Berets were

threatened with forced removal and arrest. It garnered a lot of publicity, but little else. Not long thereafter, following significant internal discord, Brown Beret leader David Sánchez disbanded the national organization (though chapters have continued operating around the country to the present day).

# 5

## Pathways to Change

THE CHICANO MOVEMENT DIDN'T JUST HAPPEN IN THE SOUTH-WEST. CHICANOS ACTIVISTS WERE EVERYWHERE! LIKE WISCONSIN, FOR INSTANCE.

As more and more Mexican Americans began to embrace Chicanismo, the Chicano Movement's ideology, they were faced with the reality of what to do with this newfound consciousness on a practical level. Whether proponents of cultural nationalism or even Marxism, some certainly advocated for a revolution—in line with other Third World liberation struggles—that would result in a Chicano homeland. As we've seen, however, most Chicano militancy called for very basic reforms within society: equitable and relevant education, an end to police brutality, fairness within the criminal justice system, and calling off an unpopular war that was taking Chicano lives in disproportionate numbers. The question for Chicano activists seeking lasting change, then, was how best to ensure that the Mexican American community gained the civil rights that had long eluded them. Many repeated the call for self-determination, the freedom for the Chicano community to make its own decisions. But did that require creating entirely new institutions (educational, economic, or political), or did it merely imply changing existing institutions so that they reflected a Chicano worldview? Chicano activists ultimately pursued two very different pathways to reform, both with significant results: higher education and the ballot box.

## CHICANAS AND CHICANOS IN HIGHER EDUCATION

The 1960s and the Baby Boom generation saw more Mexican Americans on college campuses than ever before, aided in part by War on Poverty initiatives such as the Educational Opportunity Program (EOP), which actively recruited Mexican Americans, and the GI Bill, which assisted veterans. As Mexican American college students nation-wide became politicized and formed student organizations focused on issues impacting the Mexican American community, they also began to seek ways of changing institutions of higher learning them-selves. Inspired by the implementation of Black Studies, Chicanos pushed universities to form Chicano Studies departments, which would reflect not just their culture and history but also their ethos of activism and community accountability.

In spring 1968, shortly after the East Los Angeles blowouts, Mexican American students at San José State College staged a walk-out during their commencement exercises. It was the first Chicano student protest on a college campus. That fall, students at San Francisco State College organized the Third World Liberation Front (TWLF), a mixed-minority organization that called for campus reform and the creation of a Third World College, including a Raza Studies Department. The TWLF also pushed for the admission of

THIS IS THE
ANTICOLONIAL
ANTICAPITALIST
RADICAL
CHICANO
NATIONALIST
SECTION OF MY
PERSONAL
LIBRARY.

more minority students in an open admission process. Using sit-ins, mass-meetings, and a general strike, the TWLF effort was one of the first significant examples of Chicanos uniting with other minority or Third World activists to demand change. Lasting from November 1968 to March 1969, the strike resulted in violent clashes between students and police, but it ultimately succeeded in gaining better minority recruitment and admission policies, as well as the first College of Ethnic Studies.

In January 1969, the TWLF strike spread across San Francisco Bay to UC Berkeley, where this time Mexican American students were at the forefront of the strike, along with African American, Asian American, and Native American classmates. They issued many of the same demands as their peers at San Francisco State, including a Third World College focused on understudied histories, as well as sufficient resources to carry out community-based work. The new college would also be fully controlled by students, faculty, and

THIRD WORLD
LIBERATION FRONT (TWLF)
STUDENT STRIKE

community representatives. In essence, like Chicano activists across the country, they were calling for community self-determination, but this time within the university context. Lasting several months, and sparking even more violent confrontations with law enforcement—including National Guard occupation of the campus—the strike led directly to the creation of the first Ethnic Studies Department in the country, at Berkeley.

As Chicano students forged alliances with Third World activists in Northern California, Chicano students in Southern California gathered for a conference at University of California, Santa Barbara that aimed to unify Chicano student activism and formulate a forward-thinking plan for Chicanos in higher education.

## El Plan de Santa Bárbara

In April 1969, just a month after the Chicano Youth and Liberation Conference in Denver, the Chicano Coordinating Council on Higher Education (CCHE), a network of faculty, students, and staff committed to helping Mexican American students attend colleges and universities, held a three-day conference at UC Santa

Barbara. The goal of the activists in attendance, numbering more than a hundred, was to create a plan to develop curricula and services that would help Mexican Americans gain access to and succeed in institutions of higher learning. Most of the students were undergraduates, and many had recently attended the Denver conference. Inspired by *El Plan Espiritual de Aztlán*, they saw the Santa Barbara gathering as an opportunity to implement its ideas. The new conference would indeed prove instrumental in spreading the Chicano student movement across the country, primarily through the creation of another important document of the Chicano Movement: *El Plan de Santa Bárbara*.

Like its inspiration, *El Plan de Santa Bárbara* emphasized cultural nationalism, a rejection of assimilationist pressures, and a focus on Chicano identity as a "rebirth of pride and confidence." It also advocated for self-determination, or the need to maintain community control over its own direction—in this case, in the educational arena. *El Plan de Santa Bárbara* argued that too often Mexican Americans had used their education for individual gain and had left

their communities behind in pursuit of the American Dream. As a result, the document stated, the majority of Mexican Americans were left "exploited, impoverished, and marginal." The cost of middle-class striving was simply too great, and the newfound Chicano consciousness had brought an awareness that "man is never closer to his true self as when he is close to his community." For this reason, the Santa Barbara manifesto not only acknowledged the importance of institutions of higher learning to community development, but also called for a university that responded to the needs of the community.

*El Plan de Santa Bárbara* stated that the creation of Chicano Studies represented the "total conceptualization of the Chicano community's aspirations that involve higher education." As such, it called on the State of California to implement the following: 1) proportional admission and active recruitment of Chicano students, faculty, administrators and staff; 2) a curriculum and an academic major relevant to the Chicano cultural and historical experience; 3) support and tutorial programs; 4) research programs; 5) publication programs; 6) community cultural and social action centers. Lastly, the manifesto insisted on Chicano self-determination within the university: Mexican American students, faculty, administrators, employees, and community must be "central and decisive designers of those programs."

The Santa Barbara conference and *El Plan de Santa Bárbara* were also significant in the establishment of a new student organization committed to the Chicano Movement. Student members, agreeing that both "Chicano" and "Aztlán" were essential to their new consciousness and activism, dropped their existing organizational names and unified under a new designation: Movimiento Estudiantil Chicano de Aztlán, or MEChA.

## MEChA

Organizations such as United Mexican American Students (UMAS), Mexican American Student Confederation (MASC), Mexican American Youth Association (MAYO), and Mexican American Student Association (MASA) all had been particular to specific campuses and regions, but now the new name would identify them as part of the same movement. According to Chicano scholar Carlos Muñoz, Jr., once a prominent Chicano student activist himself, the acronym MEChA meant "match" or "matchstick" and, in his words,

SYMBOLIZED THE EMERGENCE OF A NEW GENERATION
OF YOUTH, LA RAZA NUEVA, OR THE "NEW PEOPLE" OR
"REBORN YOUTH." THE ADOPTION OF THIS NEW NAME
THUS ENCOURAGED STUDENTS TO SEE THEMSELVES
AS PART OF THE NEW CHICANO/A GENERATION THAT
WAS COMMITTED TO MILITANT STRUGGLE AGAINST
US INSTITUTIONS THAT HAD HISTORICALLY BEEN
RESPONSIBLE FOR THE OPPRESSION OF MEXICAN
AMERICANS.

CHICANO STUDENT
ORGANIZATIONS
UNITE

Outlined in *El Plan de Santa Bárbara* were detailed steps that student participants in MEChA—called *MEChistas*—should follow in order to hold themselves and Chicano Studies departments accountable to the community. MEChA's first goal was precisely that: to create and maintain links between the university and the Chicano community. Thus, it would be both a student organization, responsive to the needs of student members, and a community organization, seeking alliances with local Mexican American groups and programs.

MEChA's second goal was to create a power base on campuses; it would do so by recruiting Mexican Americans and teaching them the ideology of Chicanismo—principally, the importance of giving back to one's family and community rather than serving personal advancement.

Third, MEChA would be instrumental in the creation and implementation of Chicano Studies and Chicano support services, ensuring that the programs remain vital and relevant to Chicano students. For example, MEChA members would remind "Chicano faculty and administrators where their loyalty and allegiance lies. . . . [I]t is the students who must keep after Chicano and non-Chicano administrators and faculty to see that they do not compromise the position of the students and the community." In return, MEChA would take responsibility for mobilizing community support if faculty or administrators found their jobs in jeopardy because of their commitment to student interests above their own.

The creation of MEChA, and the importance that *El Plan de Santa Bárbara* attached to students in general, underscores the central role that youth played in the Chicano Movement. It was simply vital for Chicano Studies, as an extension of the Movement, to establish itself with students at the forefront.

Expanded after the conference, *El Plan de Santa Bárbara* totaled 155 pages and was published in book form with images by Chicano

Movement artists. Much of its master plan to implement Chicano Studies programs came to fruition within the next few years. Chicano Studies, whether as an academic department, research center, or special program, was established at community colleges with large Mexican American populations, at every California state college, and on almost all the University of California campuses. It later spread throughout the Southwest, Wisconsin, Michigan, and the East Coast. Mexican American students also gained greater access to colleges and universities, and Chicano Studies programs along with MEChA helped implement many university-sponsored community initiatives.

The institutionalization of the Chicano Movement in higher education also had its challenges. Some of these were anticipated in *El Plan de Santa Bárbara*, with its repeated emphasis on the need for Chicano Studies to be rooted in the community and warning of the processes by which faculty and administrators could be co-opted by academic institutions as they sought self-advancement rather than community uplift. In a way, the emphasis revealed the writers' awareness of the contradictions and very real pressures inherent in creating a radical new discipline within a traditional structure. For example, not all Mexican American students, especially as the Chicano student movement waned, were interested in being activists or spreading Chicanismo. They became involved in other kinds of campus activities, or they focused more on career goals. For them, the notion of "defending" the Chicano community or holding Chicano Studies accountable to the community simply didn't resonate.

Similarly, Chicano faculty and administrators couldn't help but be affected by institutional pressures and academic guidelines, especially as Chicano Studies battled to establish its legitimacy as a discipline within the university. Many felt beholden to more conventional academic models and pathways. As time went on, despite the emphasis in *El Plan de Santa Bárbara* that legitimacy could come only from the Chicano community, emerging scholars, raised in academia rather than the Movement, took an approach to scholarship that didn't necessarily include grassroots community activism. Despite these challenges, *El Plan de Santa Bárbara* was instrumental in making sure that an innovative, community-based discipline with a focus on the Mexican American experience became an essential part of higher education.

# LAS HIJAS DE CUAUHTÉMOC

The Chicana feminist organization Las Hijas de Cuauhtémoc ("Daughters of Cuauhtémoc," the last Aztec ruler) began informally (and under different names) in 1968 at California State University, Long Beach. Anna Nieto-Gomez formed the group in response to Chicana activists being prevented from, or resented for, taking leadership roles in Chicano student organizations. The group also developed as a space for expressing the specific needs of Chicanas on campus and in the community, as well as a growing frustration over their limited role in the Chicano student movement.

Although women were an integral part of every aspect of the Chicano Movement, they were often relegated to the sidelines, expected to do secretarial work and cook rather than lead or act as spokespersons. Chicanas rightfully saw this as a contradiction within a civil rights movement that professed to fight for equality and justice. Chicanas grew tired of the "loyalist" versus "sellout" dichotomy and looked to historical feminist precursors for inspiration. Named after a Mexican feminist organization from the early twentieth century, Las Hijas de Cuauhtémoc found strength knowing that they were part of a long history of feminist thought and action. It published a newspaper by the same name.

# CHICANAS AND CHICANOS AT THE BALLOT BOX

One of *El Plan Espiritual de Aztlán*'s goals called for the creation of a new and independent political party, decrying the mainstream two-party system for its unresponsiveness to the Mexican American community. According to the *Plan*, Mexican Americans would attempt to "control" locations where they were a majority and to form a "pressure group" where they were a minority. Nationally, the party would be one: "La Familia de la Raza!"

Several participants left the Denver Chicano Youth Conference committed to making that political party a reality. The Raza Unida Party (RUP, or "the people united"), founded in January 1970 by José Angel Gutiérrez and Mario Compean, was local in focus at the outset and found early success in Crystal City, Texas. Its efforts showed that Mexican Americans could win elective office by advocating "brown power" and espousing a Chicano nationalist platform. The RUP eventually expanded to numerous other states as an independent third party seeking to represent the interests of the Mexican American community. Although it wasn't able to repeat its success in South Texas, the Raza Unida Party gave Chicanos valuable experience in the electoral process.

THIRD PARTY ASPIRATIONS

## La Raza Unida Party and Crystal City

The Chicano Movement's push for political power started in Crystal City, a small South Texas town where Mexican Americans were the majority but had long been governed by an Anglo minority. Most of Crystal City's 80% Mexican American population worked as migrant laborers. In 1963, led by the local packing plant's Teamsters Union and the Political Association of Spanish-Speaking Organizations from San Antonio (PASSO), five Mexican American candidates ran for city council and won, bringing nationwide attention to Crystal City. Shocked, the defeated Anglo establishment went on the offensive and resorted to dirty tactics, including firing one of the newly elected council members and cutting the pay of another in half. Los Cinco, as the new council members became known, were largely uneducated and had little political experience. As a result, they were quickly overwhelmed by the Anglo power structure, which reorganized to incorporate middle-class Mexican Americans deemed more favorable. Los Cinco were out of power within two years, but the precedent had been set. Later in the decade, as the Chicano Movement introduced young people to grassroots organizing techniques, Crystal City was looked at again as an opportunity for political mobilization.

José Angel Gutiérrez, a town native, was a junior-college student when he actively participated in the 1963 elections. The son of a doctor, he was raised relatively middle-class compared to most Mexican Americans in South Texas and was one of the few Mexican Americans allowed to attend the town's Anglo schools. When his father died, however, his family was left in poverty, and both he and his mother experienced firsthand the racism from which his social status had previously sheltered him. Always a good student, Gutiérrez attended Texas A&M University–Kingsville and later

CRYSTAL CITY ELECTIONS 1963

received a master's degree in political science from Saint Mary's College in San Antonio.

In 1967, while at Saint Mary's, Gutiérrez co-founded the hugely influential Mexican American Youth Organization (MAYO) with Mario Compean, Willie Velásquez, Ignacio Pérez, and Juan Patlán. A range of political activists influenced the group, including Corky Gonzales, Reies López Tijerina, César Chávez, and leaders of the Black Power movement. MAYO members were in attendance at the influential Alianza conference in New Mexico in October 1967, as well as the Denver Chicano Youth and Liberation Conference in March 1969. They were well-organized, and they used funds from the Office of Economic Opportunity and the War on Poverty programs to establish a number of organizations dedicated to helping the Mexican American community. Among these organizations were La Universidad de los Barrios, which sought to educate gang members and helped reduce gang conflict in San Antonio.

Articulate and charismatic, José Angel Gutiérrez didn't shy away from confrontational rhetoric. He spoke often about racist

white Texas society and, in what became an infamous speech in 1969, threatened to "Kill the Gringo." Though he later said his comment was mischaracterized—he meant that the root of Mexican American oppression was Anglo society and that it needed to be rooted out—there was no doubt that his language was inflammatory. Among the outraged parties was Mexican American Congressman Henry B. Gonzalez of

San Antonio, who felt that MAYO only spewed hatred and damaged the Mexican American cause. The firestorm created by Gutiérrez's comments prompted officials to eliminate MAYO's government and foundation funding. It also led to a split with MAYO members who sought a more moderate, less militant path; Willie Velásquez, most notably, went on to found the Southwest Voter Registration Education Project (SVREP).

José Angel Gutiérrez and Mario Compean traveled with other MAYO members to South Texas in the belief that its large Mexican American population and its history of exploitation and disenfranchisement made it ripe for political reform. In Crystal City, activists met with students

IT'S THE GRINGO WHO MAKES US DROP OUT OF SCHOOL, WHO KEEPS US IN BAD HEALTH, WHO DOESN'T PAY US GOOD WAGES, WHO PROHIBITS OUR UNIONS...

INFLAMMATORY SOUND BITE

who were frustrated by the discrimination prevalent in local schools. The long list of student grievances included bigoted teachers, a schoolwide ban on speaking Spanish, and the lack of transparency in selecting students for homecoming king and queen, cheerleading, and other honors. The student unrest had been spurred specifically by the school's cheerleading quota, which allowed only one Mexican American cheerleader despite the fact that Mexican American students comprised a majority of the school.

Diana Palacios, one of the aspiring cheerleaders, and fellow students took the issue to the school administration. A compromise was

MAYO DESCENDS UPON
CRYSTAL CITY

reached, but the administration reneged under pressure from Anglo parents. This, in turn, spurred Mexican American students to challenge other discriminatory practices. Led by 17-year-old Severita Lara, students circulated petitions with their demands, which the school board dismissed as unfounded. The students asked their parents to intervene, but they, too, faced poor treatment—which spurred more community members to support the students.

In early December 1969, with the East Los Angeles blowouts as their model, Crystal City high school students walked out of their classrooms, eventually leading to a districtwide boycott. School board officials caved in a month later, acquiescing to student demands. The victory further galvanized Crystal City's Mexican American community, showing them that they had strength in numbers and that political power was a possibility.

Building on that momentum, Gutiérrez and Compean established the Raza Unida Party and began organizing voters to challenge the

Anglo establishment. It is important to note that women played a major role in the Crystal City demonstrations, first as female students stood up for their inclusion and then as the mothers who rushed to defend their children. It set an important precedent for the RUP, which relied heavily on women organizers. Later, Martha Cotera and fellow female members created Mujeres por la Raza Unida (Women for the United People) to advocate for their inclusion in the party's decision-making process. On the ground level, women organizers effectively appealed to notions of family and the home, which proved especially important as campaigners were frequently called outside agitators, Communists, and radicals.

The RUP successfully fended off such attacks through relentless door-to-door organizing and creating an "us versus them"

EVERY YEAR IT'S THE SAME THING AND WE'RE TIRED OF IT!

CATALYST FOR A REVOLUTION

mentality—Mexicanos versus "gringos." In the next election, in spring 1970, the RUP slate in Crystal City and nearby towns won 15 of 16 school board and city council seats. Gutiérrez himself won a position on the Crystal City school board and was then named president in a reorganization. Major changes were immediately enacted in town schools: more Mexican American teachers, administrators, and staff were hired, bilingual education was implemented in early grades, and courses were taught in Mexican American history and culture to counter the dominant Anglo Texas narrative. Many Anglo families removed their children from school or moved out of town altogether.

## MALDEF

The Mexican American Legal Defense and Education Fund (MALDEF) played a key role in expanding the 1965 Voting Rights Act to include people with Spanish-surnamed citizens. Its efforts greatly increased Mexican American voter registration. Established in San Antonio, Texas, in 1968, by Pete Tijerina, MALDEF's goal was to ensure that Mexican Americans received proper legal counsel and fair treatment under the law. The organization remains very much alive and active in the 21st century.

Although the RUP continued to struggle against an entrenched establishment unwilling to cede power without a fight, its victories represented a radical change in the status quo. For years, Mexican Americans were denied political influence through the use of poll taxes, literacy tests, and gerrymandering of voter districts. Their exclusion had led to political apathy and a belief that democracy didn't extend to them. But the RUP's mobilization of Mexican American voters in South Texas gave the community and young Chicanos in particular hope that maybe the electoral process could be used to their advantage.

## The National La Raza Unida Party

By 1971–1972 the RUP had established itself in other South Texas counties. Sometimes it resorted to polarizing tactics that divided communities along racial lines; mostly it appealed to issues that impacted the Mexican American community, which had long suffered from racism, discrimination, and extreme poverty. The strategy worked, but the question was whether a platform based on ethnic solidarity could succeed at the state and national levels. Gutiérrez resisted the push to grow too quickly, believing that the party needed to further develop its base in rural South Texas. Many other members, including Compean, thought that their early successes could be replicated on a larger scale. In 1971, the RUP held its state convention in San Antonio and voted to begin organizing at the state level.

Elsewhere, Chicano activists inspired by the RUP's victories established party chapters in a number of states—most prominently in California and in Colorado, where it was led by Corky Gonzales and the Crusade for Justice, and as far away as Michigan and Wisconsin. Just south of Los Angeles, in California's 48th Congressional District, Raul Ruiz ran as an RUP candidate against Richard Alatorre, a Mexican American Democrat. In what would be a difficult situation facing the RUP and third parties in general, Ruiz won only 7% of the vote and Alatorre lost to the Republican candidate. The RUP had proved to the Democratic Party that it couldn't rely on Mexican American voter support, but it had also contributed to a victory by the GOP—a party surely less sympathetic to the Mexican American cause.

In 1972, the RUP held its national convention in El Paso, Texas. Members gathered from across the United States to debate the party's platform and direction, which was far from cohesive. The discord was represented in the vision and leadership of Corky Gonzales and José Angel Gutiérrez, who was increasingly viewed as a rising star in the Chicano Movement. Gonzales connected the RUP to

the formation of Chicano consciousness. He believed that the primary purpose of political campaigns was not to win elections but to serve as vehicles to educate the population. More than anything, he wanted the party to remain separate and immune from politicking and compromise with the two-party system. Gutiérrez was more pragmatic, calling for a focus on local issues and practical solutions. That approach was rooted in his belief that the RUP should be willing to negotiate with other parties in order to gain the most benefits for the Mexican American community.

In addition to Gonzales and Gutiérrez, Reies López Tijerina was also present at the convention, along with 1,500 delegates from throughout the Southwest and Midwest. What started as an exciting dialogue in the pursuit of party influence became, in the end, a power struggle between Gonzales and Gutiérrez over who was to be national chairman. A dispute developed over how to vote for the chairman, whether by individual votes or by delegate blocks. Popular vote was the ultimate decision, and Gutiérrez emerged as the victor. Although both men embraced on stage and called for unity, it was clear that the divisions were great and that the ideological differences between chapters and leaders would make consensus difficult. No national structure was ever implemented.

The RUP faced an uphill battle. In Texas, six statewide candidates were nominated, including Ramsey Muñiz, a charismatic 29-year-old lawyer and former college football star, for governor; Alma Canales for lieutenant governor, and Maria Jimenez for attorney general. In total, the RUP fielded candidates in more than 40 Texas counties. In the November general election, despite major voter registration initiatives, all RUP candidates lost. In California, despite a concerted effort and the expenditure of significant resources, the RUP failed to collect the required number of signatures to appear on the state ballot.

Not least of all, the RUP failed to achieve anything resembling

an ideological consensus. In large part this had to do with regional differences, but it also reflected ideological differences within the Chicano Movement as a whole. The emphasis on self-determination looked differently in Mexican American South Texas than it did in such urban centers as Los Angeles or the Bay Area, where Mexican Americans found it difficult to build a strategy based on cultural nationalism. Others wanted a party platform that focused on class issues and critiqued capitalism rather than one built on ethnic solidarity. Still others saw the third-party initiative as a quixotic quest and felt that energies should be focused elsewhere.

Despite its setbacks, the Raza Unida Party's success in South Texas can't be overstated. In a region where Mexican Americans had been governed by Anglo minority rule for over a century, the RUP demonstrated that through effective organizing, education, and resistance in the face of intimidation, Mexican Americans could have a real impact in the voting booth. And though the party generally struggled at the state level, its presence changed the political land-scape in Texas and encouraged a generation of Chicanos to become active in the political process. The two-party system proved too pow-erful to budge, but no longer could the Anglo establishment ignore or rely on the acquiescence of the Mexican American community.

At the national level, the RUP also struggled to find its footing, but the party's formation demonstrated the political ambitions of the Chicano Movement. Many Chicanos wanted cultural nation-alism to be more than mere rhetoric—not just pride in one's cul-ture, history, and values without substance; they wanted it to be the basis for profound change in society. Unsatisfied with simply pro-testing against power, more and more Chicanos felt it was also their right to wield power.

# 6

## The Chicano Cultural Renaissance

One of the central and most enduring elements of the Chicano Movement was the cultural activity that the political struggle inspired. As Chicanos sought to define Chicanismo, they turned to poets and artists to create the imagery and language of this new identity and bring it to life. In the mid-to-late 1960s, as the quest for Chicano cultural identity was gaining urgency, Corky Gonzales's epic poem *I am Joaquín* became the anthem for the Chicano Movement, and Alurista and fellow poets used the concept of Aztlán, the mythical homeland of the Aztecs, to forge a notion of a Chicano homeland. In both cases, politics and culture were intertwined. We have also seen how Luis Valdez and Teatro Campesino used theater as a labor organizing tool, laying the groundwork for a politically engaged arts movement.

At the same time, newspapers, magazines, and journals sprang up around the country that gave artists and writers an important venue for their work. These publications shed light on news and events relevant to the Chicano community, but they also were ways for Chicano activists to network and dialogue with one another. Long before the Internet age, small regional newspapers and magazines with little to no budget provided a way for activists to inform others around the country that the Chicano Movement was larger than any one place. These publications often featured poetry, fiction, and visual arts, and soon a distinctive Chicano voice began to emerge. The expressions of that voice and that artistic vision became known as the Chicano Renaissance.

## NEWSPAPERS, MAGAZINES, AND JOURNALS

Hundreds of publications emerged in the late 1960s and early 1970s, some lasting one issue, others that continue to the present day. In addition to the UFW's newspaper, *El Malcriado*, and *El Grito del*

## Chicano Press | Association

*Norte* in New Mexico, Cuban American activist Eliezer Risco, along with Joe Razo and Raul Ruiz, published *La Raza* in Los Angeles. *La Raza* played an important role in the 1968 student mobilization there and was an inspiration to other student newspapers. The Brown Beret's had their own publication, *La Causa*, which was used to recruit new members and raise awareness about police brutality. The Crusade for Justice published *El Gallo*, and *Inferno* was an important newspaper out of San Antonio, Texas, that included staff from the Raza Unida Party. Chicano newspapers understood that the mainstream press generally ignored Mexican American issues; with the exception of Ruben Salazar in the *Los Angeles Times*, whatever press Chicanos did receive was rarely sympathetic. Chicano publishers sought to fill the void themselves, forming the Chicano Press Association in 1968. Over 50 newspapers were represented at the association's first conference in Albuquerque, New Mexico.

Founded in Los Angeles in 1967, *Con Safos: Reflections of Life in the Barrio* was one of the first Chicano magazines. Its tone was proud and unapologetic for its bicultural, bilingual stance—staffers even joked about its shoestring budget and sporadic publishing schedule. *Con Safos*, a term loosely meaning "back at you" and used by graffiti writers to ward off defacement, introduced readers to Chicano fiction, poetry, artwork, and photography. It also included a humorous lexicon of life in the barrio. Sergio Hernandez's "Arnie and Porfi" cartoons became a staple of the magazine, and movement lawyer's Oscar Zeta Acosta's novel *The Autobiography of a Brown Buffalo* (1972) was first published in *Con Safos* in serialized form.

Perhaps the most influential Movement periodical of all was *El Grito: A Journal of Contemporary Mexican-American Thought*, established in 1967 in Berkeley, California, by Octavio I. Romano-V., Nick C. Vaca, and Andrés Ybarra. The journal began as an academic quarterly focused on the social sciences, publishing emerging scholarship on the Mexican American community. But it had its biggest impact with two influential anthologies: *El Espejo,* which featured fiction and poetry from the Movement's most important writers; and *Voices*, a compilation of influential essays. *El Grito* also dedicated issues to visual artists, including members of the Bay Area–based Mexican American Liberation Art Front (MALAF). Both *El Espejo* and *Voices* were used extensively in nascent Chicano Studies programs and became the foundation for the first Chicano publishing house in the country, Editorial Quinto Sol (Fifth Sun), which gave Chicano authors a much-needed venue to publish their work.

Quinto Sol

RIVERA
ANAYA
HINOJOSA
Portillo TRAMBLEY

1967 - 1974
BIRTH OF CHICANO
PUBLISHING

Editorial Quinto Sol brought national attention to some of the most seminal works of Chicano literature.

*El Grito* and Quinto Sol were followed by a number of other Chicano-focused publications, including *Aztlán* (Los Angeles, 1970), *Revista Chicano-Riqueña* (Indiana, 1973), and the *Bilingual Review* (New York, 1970). Independent Chicano publishing houses focused exclusively on Mexican American and Latino writers soon emerged, most notably Pajarito Publications, Bilingual Press, and Arte Público Press. Some of the most well-known Chicano authors, including Sandra Cisneros, Ana Castillo, and Victor Villaseñor, first published their work with these presses. Women also formed important journals and anthologies dedicated exclusively to Chicana feminist thought and expression, such as *Encuentro Femenil*, the first journal of Chicana scholarship.

# LITERATURE

## QUINTO SOL PRIZE

As the first independent publishing house devoted to Chicano literature, Editorial Quinto Sol established the Quinto Sol Prize in 1970
to help promote Mexican American authors and literary nationalism. The first prize was awarded in 1971 to Tomás Rivera for *...y
no se lo tragó la tierra/...and the earth did not devour him*. This short
experimental novel, written in Spanish but published with a trans-
lation, details the life of a young migrant field worker as his family follows the harvest from Texas northward through the Midwest.
Brutal in its depiction of poverty and the exploitation suffered by
migrant workers, the novel is also a coming-of-age story, as the
young protagonist questions religion and the accepted values of

TOMÁS RIVERA'S
...AND THE EARTH
DID NOT DEVOUR
HIM

his elders, confronts racism and discrimination, and through it all, reveals the desperate hope and perseverance of his community. This was Rivera's only novel. Raised in Crystal City, Texas, he became a highly respected educator and the first Chicano chancellor of the University of California, Riverside.

The second Quinto Sol Prize was awarded in 1972 to Rudolfo Anaya for *Bless Me, Última*, one of the most widely read books in all of Chicano literature. Anaya's story draws strongly from the Indo-Hispano culture and history of his native New Mexico. Antonio, the young boy at the center of the narrative, is torn between his mother's desire that he become a Catholic priest and his father's desire that he become a vaquero of the *llano,* the land. An elderly healer, Última, comes to live with the family and shows Antonio that he need not choose between these disparate paths; instead she shows the boy that his history is a synthesis of Catholicism and indigenous myth and custom. Antonio must learn to accept and embrace the complexities of both as an all-encompassing identity. Through strong symbolism, the novel alludes to many of the Movement's ideas about Aztlán as a spiritual homeland for Chicanos.

RUDOLFO ANAYA'S BLESS ME, ULTIMA

The third Quinto Sol Prize was awarded in 1973 to Rolando Hinojosa's *Estampas del Valle y Otras Obras/Sketches of the Valley and Other Works,* the first of many of Hinojosa's books set in a fictional county in the lower Rio Grande Valley of Texas.

The works of Rivera, Anaya, and Hinojosa formed the vanguard of Chicano literature. Their novels, written in Spanish, English, and a mix of the two, showed Chicanos that it was possible to write about complex Mexican American characters, to set those characters in the landscape that was most familiar to them, and to present an unabashedly Chicano worldview without fear of alienating or confusing the reader.

In 1975, Quinto Sol awarded its final award to Estella Portillo Trambley for her short story collection, *Rain of Scorpions.* Though not as well known as her predecessors' works, her collection marked an important shift in Chicano literature. From the late 1970s on, more and more women published their writing and began to counter the male-dominated narrative established by early-Movement authors and editors.

## Defining Chicano Literature

As Chicano authors found their way into print, almost immediately there was a need to define Chicano literature. Questions of language and idiom arose: should Chicano authors write in Spanish or in a mix of Spanish and English and to what extent did that decision determine their audience? Should Chicano authors write exclusively for the Mexican American community or should they seek to appeal and possibly educate a larger audience? And did Chicano authors have a responsibility to depict a Chicano worldview? Rivera, Anaya, and Hinojosa's themes of overcoming hardship and racism, the resilience of the Mexican American community, and a connection to the earth, laid a foundation that fit the Movement's desire to emphasize the beauty and strength of the Chicano community. Other works struggled to find their place.

José Antonio Villarreal's *Pocho,* originally published in 1959 and rereleased in 1970 in response to the growing interest in the lives of Mexican Americans, is the coming-of-age story of a Mexican

Á LA MAGU

OSCAR ZETA ACOSTA'S THE AUTOBIOGRAPHY OF A BROWN BUFFALO

American boy caught between two cultures who ultimately rejects many aspects of his family and community in his quest to become a writer. The novel, written before the Chicano Movement, was heavily criticized for its apparently Mexican-American, or "assimilationist" stance. Oscar Zeta Acosta, who gained prominence as the attorney for the East Los Angeles 13, published two semi-autobiographical novels, *The Autobiography of a Brown Buffalo* (1972) and *The Revolt of the Cockroach People* (1973), which detail the narrator's anguished quest to understand his identity as well as his participation in the 1970 Chicano Moratorium. But the decidedly in-your-face anti-hero stance of Acosta's fictional self, including rampant drug use, derogatory descriptions of just about everyone (but especially women), made many in the community uncomfortable with casting his work as representative of Chicano literature. Similarly, John Rechy's 1963 novel, *City of Night*, about a Mexican American youth's entry into gay subculture, was often overlooked as part of the early Chicano canon despite its importance in American literature.

# POETRY

Chicano poetry was the most widespread literary form, appearing in newspapers and performed at Movement rallies and meetings. It was often the most politically driven as well, at times bordering on slogans in verse. But Chicano poets also articulated the Chicano Movement's most complex ideas—the contradictions of embracing divergent or opposing cultures, and synthesizing what remained at odds, whether that was language, history, or the worldview of Chicanos vis-à-vis mainstream American society. In his book *Chicano Authors*, the early Chicano literary critic Juan Bruce-Novoa characterized Chicano poetry as "protest literature" that reflected the following:

> LAMENT AND ANGER OVER THE CHICANOS' VIRTUES AND TALENTS BEING IGNORED, WASTED, OR DELIBERATELY SUPPRESSED BY THE MAJORITY SOCIETY; THE RECALLING OF MEXICAN HISTORY, MYTHOLOGY, AND POPULAR LORE; EMPHASIS ON THE FAMILY, WITH ROOTS IN THE LAND OR THE BARRIO; THE PACHUCO AS A PRECURSOR TO CHICANO CULTURAL AWARENESS; THE OPPOSITION OF CHICANO ORAL HISTORY—"TRUTH"—TO UNITED STATES WRITTEN HISTORY—"LIES"; THE OPPOSITION OF CHICANOS' HUMANISM AND HARMONY WITH NATURE TO THE TECHNOLOGICAL, AHUMANISTIC, UNECOLOGICAL UNITED STATES SOCIETY, THE OPPOSITION OF CHICANO (MESTIZO) ETHNIC, CULTURAL, AND RACIAL OPENNESS TO THE ANGLO AMERICANS' RESISTANCE AND HOSTILITY TO OUTSIDERS.

Corky Gonzales, Alurista, Abelardo Delgado, Tino Villanueva, and Reyes Cárdenas were early representatives of this thrust, as was José Montoya, whose poem "El Louie" was an elegy for a tragic pachuco figure that employed *caló,* pachuco slang, to reveal a complex interior world rife with contradictions and beauty. Raúl Salinas and Ricardo Sánchez, both former prisoners, wrote with raw anger and passion about barrio and pinto (prison) life, as well as their politicization as Chicanos. Following closely on their heels, women poets

FESTIVAL DE FLOR Y CANTO

such as Bernice Zamora, Angela de Hoyos, Lorna Dee Cervantes, Evangelina Vigil, Alma Villanueva, Carmen Tafolla, and Lucha Corpi posited verse as personal as it was political, voicing female concerns and perspectives, and in doing so expanded the scope and very definition of Chicano poetry.

Beginning in 1973, in Los Angeles, Festival de Flor y Canto (Festival of Flower and Song) brought together some of the most important writers of the Chicano Movement to read their work and exchange ideas. Subsequent festivals throughout the 1970s were held in Austin, San Antonio, Albuquerque, and Tempe, Arizona. These events, like the literary publications focused on Chicano output, gave writers the opportunity to discuss the important themes and motivations of their work. In the process, a growing network of writers, cultural critics, and activists contributed to the creation of a unique literary tradition.

# ART

Student activists at the 1969 Chicano Youth and Liberation Conference in Denver understood the importance of the arts to political mobilization. In *El Plan Espiritual de Aztlán*, one of the seven goals specifically called for artists to create work that culturally empowered the Mexican American community. Activists wrote that the "cultural values of our people strengthen our identity and moral backbone of the movement. Our culture unites and educates the family of La Raza towards liberation with one heart and mind." With this important charge, Chicano artists set out to create work that responded to the needs of a community that had not previously been exposed to art, or at least not the kind found in art history books, museums, galleries, or other cultural institutions.

From the outset, Chicano artists sought ways to bring art to the people and reach as wide an audience as possible. They did

so primarily through two important mediums that came to define Chicano Art: the mural and the silkscreen poster. Artists also sought to create community art centers (or *centros*) where people could gather for cultural events and celebrations as well as political meetings. Along with these centers, arts collectives emerged where like-minded artists could collaborate on creative projects, raise funds, and support one another's artistic endeavors.

Perhaps even more so than Chicano poets, visual artists gave Chicanos imagery that they could immediately identify with the pride they felt in their new identity. This included images from pre-Columbian history and myth, such as Aztec warriors, pyramids, and Mesoamerican symbols; historical Mexican figures such as Emiliano Zapata, Pancho Villa, La Adelita, and social reformer Ricardo Flores Magón; and symbols from the Chicano Movement such as César Chávez, Dolores Huerta, and the farmworker eagle. Wherever they looked in their barrios—a mural painted on a storefront wall or a poster stapled to a telephone poll—Mexican Americans were able to find imagery that addressed them directly, instilling cultural pride and encouraging them to fight against injustice.

## THE MURAL

Chicano artists found an important precedent for politically engaged public art in the famous Mexican muralists of the first half of the twentieth century. Beginning shortly after the Mexican Revolution in the 1920s, Diego Rivera, José Clemente Orozco, and David Alfaro Siqueiros—known as *los tres grandes*—painted monumental murals, most of them commissioned by the government, to recreate the history of Mexico. Staunchly leftist, the Mexican muralists saw their work as a revolutionary tool that could teach and potentially transform the mostly illiterate Mexican masses.

Beginning in the late 1960s, Chicano artists borrowed from the imagery and confrontational style of the Mexican muralists. But instead of large government or private commissions, most Chicano muralists painted with whatever supplies that they had—often house paint—and on whatever walls were available, without consideration for weather conditions or sun exposure. (As a result, most of the early murals are now gone). Although some artists developed into masters of their craft, most of the muralists were novices and the

RIVERA

SIQUEIROS

OROZCO

CHICANO PARK — SAN DIEGO, CA

murals were spontaneous creations, often crudely painted, with an emphasis on the political message rather than the aesthetics.

Antonio Bernal's 1968 mural in Del Rey, California, painted on the side of the UFW Teatro Campesino Cultural Center, was one of the first Chicano murals. Although simple in design, it presented some of the core themes and central figures that would be replicated in hundreds of murals in the following decades. In addition to a pre-Columbian image of Bonampak, an ancient Mayan city, Bernal painted a series of Mexican and Mexican American heroes (La Adelita, Villa, Zapata, and Joaquín Murrieta) marching alongside contemporary civil rights activists (César Chávez, Reies López Tijerina, Malcolm X, and Martin Luther King, Jr.).

Chicano muralists soon became active across the country. Another early work, Mario Castillo's 1968 *Metafísica,* was painted in Chicago, where eventually the arts collective Movimiento Artístico Chicano (MARCH) sponsored a number of mural projects. In the Southwest, Artes Guadalupanos de Aztlán was an active mural collective that created almost 20 murals in Santa Fe, New Mexico; Denver, Colorado; and Phoenix, Arizona.

One of the most important Chicano mural sites in the United States is Chicano Park in San Diego's Barrio Logan. Painted on the concrete underpass of the Coronado Bridge, the murals were the result of intensive community action to thwart the building of a California Highway Patrol headquarters on land that had been designated as a park. On April 22, 1970, community members, already frustrated that the newly built Coronado Bridge bisected their neighborhood, occupied the underpass area, and, with tools from home, began constructing the parks themselves. Eventually the City of San Diego granted almost eight acres to park use, and community activists sought to turn the newly established Chicano Park into a vibrant cultural center. Artist Salvador Torres suggested that murals be painted on the concrete pillars that dominate the park, and in 1973, San Diego artists, many of them members of an arts collective called Toltecas en Aztlán, commenced painting. In subsequent years, Chicano artists from Los Angeles and Sacramento joined the effort to paint dozens of murals depicting Chicano history, culture, and community activism.

Los Angeles and the San Francisco Mission District also became important mural centers. In 1973, San Francisco artists transformed Balmy Alley into an internationally renowned mural site. That same year, Patricia Rodriguez and Graciela Carrillo formed Mujeres Muralistas (Women Muralists), an arts collective that painted numerous murals in the Mission District. Susan Cervantes, a member of Mujeres Muralistas, later founded Precita Eyes Mural Center, a community-based organization in San Francisco dedicated to supporting and promoting mural projects.

Los Angeles, with the largest concentration of Mexican Americans in the country, is also home to the largest concentration of Chicano murals. In 1973, the Mechicano Art Center organized the painting of 20 murals in the Ramona Gardens Housing Project, and two years

JUDY BACA'S GREAT WALL OF LOS ANGELES

later, Goez Gallery organized a similar project in the Estrada Courts Housing Project. Some of the most important names in Chicano Art from Los Angeles—including Wayne Alaniz Healy, Willie Herrón, Gilbert "Magu" Lujan, Carlos Almaraz, Frank Romero, and Gronk— participated in these projects. But it was Judy Baca, a young muralist, who undertook the most ambitious mural project in the country: *The Great Wall of Los Angeles.*

With numerous public art projects already under her belt, Baca began preparations for the mural in 1974. Working in a flood-control channel from 1976 through 1983, she joined with hundreds of youth and volunteers to depict a "revised" history of California, documenting in almost 3,000 feet of painting the overlooked histories of the state's marginalized populations.

In 1976, Judy Baca also founded the Social Public Art Resource Center (SPARC) to fund, support, and promote muralism. Her *Great Wall*, along with murals in San Francisco's Balmy Alley and Chicano Park in San Diego, showed artists taking ownership not only of public space and their communities, but also portraying and promoting alternative histories. It was an active art form, engaged and direct, but more than anything else, the murals turned drab buildings into colorful canvases and working-class neighborhoods into vibrant art spaces.

## THE POSTER

Similar to the mural, the silkscreen poster was perfect for bringing art out of museums and galleries and into the community. Likewise, Chicano artists also found inspiration in Mexican artists and Mexican art movements, such as José Guadalupe Posada, whose *calavera* (skull) prints depicted and critiqued the whole range of pre-revolutionary Mexican society. The Mexican print collective Taller de Gráfica Popular, founded in the late 1930s, provided

another example of socially engaged artists coming together in common cause. In Mexico and elsewhere, printmaking and its ability to create multiples to better propagate one's message had long been tied to political activism, and this was especially true of the silkscreen poster.

With a relatively simple, inexpensive set-up, a silkscreen printmaker can produce hundreds of multiples for distribution. From the early days of the Chicano Movement, the silkscreen poster was used to support political action, raise awareness about issues, and

inspire people to become involved. Countless posters were made to support the United Farm Worker's grape boycott, such as Xavier Viramontes's classic *Boycott Grapes*, which features an Aztec warrior crushing grapes, or Andrew Zermeño's *Huelga!*, which depicts a farmworker in motion waving the UFW flag. Often these beautiful, multicolored posters included calls for action as well as information about where an event or rally was to be held.

The Royal Chicano Air Force (RCAF), an arts collective based in Sacramento, California, often worked with César Chávez and the UFW to produce posters for marches and other cam-

BARRIO
GALLERY

paigns. In 1968, during the Third World Liberation Front (TWLF) strike at San Francisco State College and UC Berkeley, Chicano artists like Rupert Garcia and Malaquias Montoya created iconic images in support of the students' demands. They also created posters protesting the Vietnam War and in support of Third World liberation movements, which made the important connection between student activism and other freedom struggles around the world.

Numerous print collectives developed out of this intense period of poster production and formed print *talleres*, or workshops, and art centers. In 1970, Sister Karen Boccalero established Selp Help Graphics and Arts in East Los Angeles to teach silkscreen printmaking and to provide cultural experiences for the local community. With much the same mission, artists in San Francisco founded La Raza Silkscreen Center in 1971.

Although many Chicano artists also utilized other mediums, the silkscreen poster became closely identified with the Chicano Movement, in part because it was so easy to disseminate. Community organizations had the same posters displayed on their walls; participants at rallies and other events took them home. Thus, as sociologist George Lipsitz puts it, silkscreen posters "nurtured and sustained collective memory by commemorating important moments of struggle in Mexican and Mexican American History."

# RASQUACHISMO

*Rasquache*, loosely meaning "to make do without," is a term that has been closely associated with Chicano Art. In his seminal essay on the subject, Chicano cultural critic Tomás Ybarra-Frausto described rasquachismo as "an underdog perspective—a view from *los de abajo*, an attitude rooted in resourcefulness and adaptability, yet mindful of stance and style." With limited resources at their disposal, Chicano artists often employed rasquachismo to realize their creative vision. Chicano Park in San Diego is a good example of this sensibility, as artists transformed cement pillars into beautiful murals.

## COMMUNITY ART CENTERS AND COLLECTIVES

The Chicano Art Movement was as much about artists working together as it was about the accomplishments of any one artist. Guided by many of the same goals, artists sought each other out, and many formed important collectives that both cultivated innovative creative projects and supported artists' endeavors. Important art centers include many that still exist today, such as the Galería de la Raza (1970) in San Francisco's Mission District and Centro Cultural de la Raza (1970) in San Diego, which used an abandoned facility in Balboa Park to create an art studio and performing arts center. Casa Aztlán in Chicago and Guadalupe Cultural Arts Center in San Antonio, Texas, point to the widespread nature of these creative collaborations.

Sometimes artists came together simply to discuss their role as Chicano artists; in other instances they continued for years to produce art collectively or as arts activist organizations. One of the most important collectives was the short-lived Mexican American Liberation Art Front (MALAF) in the Bay Area, which met from 1968 to 1970, and included Manuel Hernandez-Trujillo, Esteban Villa, René Yañez, and Malaquias Montoya, all key contributors to the Chicano Art Movement. Asco (Spanish for nausea) was a Los Angeles arts collective formed in 1971 that included Patssi Valdez, Willie Herrón, Gronk, and Harry Gamboa, Jr. Ahead of its time, the group employed experimental performance art to critique the art world, pop culture, and even Chicano culture. In 1972, José Montoya and Esteban Villa founded the Rebel Chicano Art Front, but after confusion with the acronym of the Royal Canadian Air Force, the Sacramento-based group decided to embrace the confusion and changed its name to the Royal Chicano Air Force. Intertwining humor, satire, and cultural production, the RCAF was deeply committed to ways in which the arts could inform community activism.

In San Antonio, Texas, Con Safo and later Los Quemados brought together some of the most important names in Chicano Art, such as Mel Casas, Felipe Reyes, César Martínez, Santa Barraza, Carmen Lomas Garza, and Amado Peña. In Los Angeles, Carlos Almaraz, Magú, Roberto de la Rocha, and Frank Romero made up Los Four. These two collectives featured some of the first Chicano artists to exhibit in mainstream institutions, which was at once a milestone and an indicator that the Chicano Art Movement had begun to shift from its community-focused origins and set its sights on acceptance into the mainstream art world.

# DRAMA AND FILM

Teatro Campesino remains the most well-known Chicano theater group; its actos, such as *Las Dos Caras del Patroncito* (1965), *Los Vendidos* (1967), and *Pensamiento Serpentino* (1973) inspired theater groups around the country to write and perform their own. In 1970, Teatro Campesino organized the First Annual Festival de los Teatros Chicanos (Festival of Chicano Theaters), which was attended by sixteen theater troupes. By 1976, more than a hundred *teatros* performed around the country and five teatro festivals were organized. Teatros Nacional de Aztlán (TENAZ, National Theater of Aztlán) was established to support Chicano dramatic efforts. Most theater troupes initially adopted the form of the acto because of its directness and relatively simple production, but soon groups began to develop longer and more elaborate productions, such as Teatro de la Esperanza's 1974 play, *Guadalupe*, which detailed social strife in the eponymous small town. The play toured the country as well as Mexico, and represented a push among Chicano teatros toward professional companies.

In 1978, Teatro Campesino produced *Zoot Suit*, which premiered at the Mark Taper Forum in Los Angeles and set attendance records. The following year the play appeared on Broadway and was later made into a successful film. Starring actor Edward James Olmos in one of his first major roles, and Luis Valdez's brother, Daniel Valdez, *Zoot Suit* is based on the 1942 Sleepy Lagoon murder trial in Los

DANZA AZTECA

TEATRO

BALLET FOLKLORICO

Angeles and the media's demonization of Mexican American youth that culminated in the 1943 Zoot Suit Riots. Like other Chicano Movement resuscitations of the pachuco, *Zoot Suit* views its subject as a courageous countercultural figure ahead of his time, a victim of racist American society, and solidly in the pantheon of Chicano heroes.

The Chicano Movement also inspired a new wave of Chicano film-makers, including Jesús Salvador Treviño, Paul Espinoza, Gregory Nava, Moctesuma Esparza, and Sylvia Morales. Luis Valdez and Teatro Campesino also experimented with film, most notably their 1969 adaptation of *I am Joaquín*. Due to the high production cost of feature-length movies, many budding filmmakers whet their teeth on smaller documentary projects in the early 1970s; full-length releases came in the late '70s and early '80s. In 1972, Treviño made a nation-ally televised documentary called *Yo soy chicano (I am Chicano)*, which documented the Chicano Movement. In 1977, he filmed one of the first feature-length movies, *Raices de Sangre*, which tells the story of a Harvard educated Chicano lawyer who returns to his hometown on the Texas-Mexico border and becomes involved in the struggle of sweatshop workers. Efraín Gutiérrez's *Please, Don't Bury Me Alive* (1976), recently recovered and re-released, is considered the first Chicano feature-length film, and details a young Chicano coming to terms with his brother's death in Vietnam. Later nota-ble releases include films inspired by early works of Chicano liter-ature such as *The Ballad of Gregorio Cortez* (1982) and *…And the Earth Did Not Swallow Him* (1995), based on Tomás Rivera's novel.

## MUSIC AND DANCE

Dancers and musicians also contributed to the Chicano Renaissance. Folkloric dance groups sprouted up around the country and per-formed at movement meetings and festivals. Mexican *folklórico* and Danza Azteca were popular because they emphasized cultural pride and were a popular way of teaching Mexican Americans about their heritage. Chicano musicians also expressed themselves through a wide variety of genres. Teatro Campesino and other theater troupes adopted corridos to tell stories of Chicano Movement events and figures. Lalo Guerrero, a well-known Mexican American musician since the 1940s, became popular again among Chicano artists who saw him as a generational bridge. Guerrero wrote much of the score for Valdez's play and film *Zoot Suit*. Chicano rock groups also became popular; these included El Chicano, Malo, and Tierra—but none achieved more acclaim than Santana.

WRITING IS DANGEROUS BECAUSE WE ARE AFRAID OF WHAT THE WRITING REVEALS: THE FEARS, THE ANGERS, THE STRENGTHS OF A WOMAN UNDER A TRIPLE OR QUADRUPLE OPPRESSION. — GLORIA ANZALDÚA

## A SILENT VOICE EMERGES

In her 1971 article "Women: New Voice of La Raza," written in response to the first National Chicana Women's Conference (Conferencia de Mujeres por la Raza) in Houston, Texas, Mirta Vidal explained the layered oppressions of Chicanas in the following terms:

THE OPPRESSION SUFFERED BY CHICANAS IS DIFFERENT FROM THAT SUFFERED BY MOST WOMEN IN THIS COUNTRY. BECAUSE CHICANAS ARE PART OF AN OPPRESSED NATIONALITY, THEY ARE SUBJECTED TO THE RACISM PRACTICED AGAINST LA RAZA. SINCE THE OVERWHELMING MAJORITY OF CHICANOS ARE WORKERS, CHICANAS ARE ALSO VICTIMS OF THE EXPLOITATION OF THE WORKING CLASS. BUT IN ADDITION, CHICANAS, ALONG WITH THE REST OF WOMEN, ARE RELEGATED TO AN INFERIOR POSITION BECAUSE OF THEIR SEX. THUS, RAZA WOMEN SUFFER A TRIPLE FORM OF OPPRESSION: AS MEMBERS OF AN OPPRESSED NATIONALITY, AS WORKERS, AND AS WOMEN.

From the outset of the Chicano Movement, Chicana feminists argued not only for their inclusion, but also for recognition that asking for gender equality was not an effort to divide the Movement but to call attention to all layers of injustice—whether perpetrated by Anglo American society or from within the Chicano community. By the late 1970s, Chicana writers, artists, scholars, and activists began to introduce this awareness into Chicano intellectual and cultural activity, and by the mid-1980s, Chicana feminists had brought issues of gender and sexuality to the forefront. Contrasting with the Chicano Movement's nationalist rhetoric, in which sweeping themes of *carnalismo* (brotherhood), *la familia* (the family), La Raza (the people), and Aztlán permeated the discussion, Chicana writers explored the body, their emotional life, and oppression within the home. While so-called "women's issues" such as contraception and abortion were often considered less important than issues of racism and class exploitation, Chicana writers used the personal, day-to-day experience of their lives to carve out and further complicate understandings of Chicano identity.

In 1981, two pioneering Chicana lesbian-feminists and activists, Gloria Anzaldúa and Cherríe Moraga, edited the landmark anthology *This Bridge Called My Back: Writings by Radical Women of Color*, which gave women writers the opportunity to explore feminism in the context of their respective cultures. In her 1980 essay "Speaking in Tongues: A Letter to Third World Women Writers," Anzaldúa warns of separating the political and the personal; in fact, she argues, the strength of women's writing rests in their particular "feminine" view of the world. "What validates us as human beings validates us as writers," she explains. "We must use what is important to us to get to the writing. *No topic is too trivial.*" Too often Chicanas had remained silent or had been silenced by others through language that dismissed or belittled issues facing women of color. But books such as *This Bridge Called My Back* became important vehicles for opening up Chicana feminist discourse about the intersection of race, class, and gender. The volume was also notable for expressing solidarity with other Latinas and Third World women.

Other important Chicana feminist writings soon followed. Moraga published *Loving in the War Years* (1983), a combination of autobiographical essays and poetry that addressed her bicultural upbringing, her identity as a lesbian and a Chicana, and her relationship with her mother. Sandra Cisneros's landmark novel, *The House on Mango Street* (1984), tells the story of Esperanza, a young girl growing up in a working-class Chicago neighborhood, but it's just as much about the lives of the women who surround her. Taught in countless high school and college classrooms, Cisneros's novel is perhaps the most widely read book in all of Chicano literature.

Ana Castillo's experimental epistolary novel, *The Mixquiahuala Letters* (1986), explores identity, male oppression, and the fraught friendship of two independent women. She later tackled Chicana

SHE'S SO COURAGEOUS.

feminism head-on in her book *Massacre of the Dreamers: Essays on Xicanisma* (1994). Other women writers of note who began publishing in the 1980s include Denise Chávez, Helena Maria Viramontes, and Alicia Gaspar de Alba.

The most influential book to emerge out of this wave of Chicana feminist writers is undoubtedly Anzaldúa's semi-autobiographical *Borderlands/La Frontera*. Published in 1987, the work mixes multiple genres from poetry to theoretical essay. Critical of Anglo domination and attempts to strip Chicanos of their culture, Anzaldúa is equally critical of male domination within the Chicano community, as well as discrimination toward gays and lesbians. She finds strength in the *mestizaje*, the hybridity of experience, at the same time that she recognizes the pain that can result from these clashes. The "borderlands" in the title are the multiple borders that exist in our lives between genders, cultures, languages, nations; Anzaldúa sees them as rich sites of cultural experience. She also turns her gaze on indigenous spirituality and myth to develop the idea of a "new mestiza consciousness" that will break down debilitating cultural, sexual, and gender barriers. Although *Borderlands* appeared long after the wane of Chicano Movement activism in the early to mid-1970s, Anzaldúa embraces and expands many of the key ideas that emerged out of the Chicano Movement, including indigenous myth, the notion of a spiritual homeland, cultural pride, and calls to fight oppression and injustice wherever they may be found.

# Conclusion:
## DECLINE AND LEGACY

The Chicano Movement, like other counterculture and protest movements of the 1960s that continued into the early 1970s, began to decline with the end of the Vietnam War in 1975. The main thrusts of the movement—César Chávez and the farmworkers' struggle, Reies López Tijerina and the Alianza, Corky Gonzales and the Crusade for Justice, José Angel Gutiérrez and the Raza Unida Party, and youth militancy exemplified by the Brown Berets—lost momentum as the attention of the nation turned away from radical politics and collective action.

Despite significant victories, the United Farm Workers struggled to keep contracts as they battled the Teamsters Union. Internal dissent over the direction of the UFW, including questions about Chávez's leadership, weakened the union, and by the 1990s its contracts covered only about 10,000 workers. The hiring of undocumented workers often undermined unionization efforts; as a result, the UFW advocated for restrictive immigration policies, which placed them at odds with other Mexican American activists. The union survives today, but barely. Many of the conditions strikers fought against 50 years ago remain unchanged, and most agricultural workers are undocumented immigrants—a vulnerable and exploited population with few protections.

The Alianza land grant movement in New Mexico also floundered once Tijerina was released from prison in 1971. Unable to hold a leadership position in the Alianza for five years due to the conditions of his parole, Tijerina organized other land grant efforts far more conciliatory in tone, emphasizing a philosophy of "Brotherhood Awareness." Many followers were uninspired by this change. When he returned to the Alianza leadership in 1976, the organization was too splintered to save.

Farther north, in Denver, the Crusade for Justice also suffered the effects of internal discord and police confrontations. Members were frequently harassed and jailed. In 1973, a shootout broke out

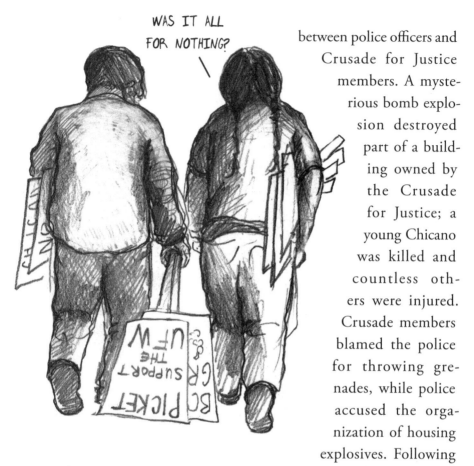

WAS IT ALL FOR NOTHING?

between police officers and Crusade for Justice members. A mysterious bomb explosion destroyed part of a building owned by the Crusade for Justice; a young Chicano was killed and countless others were injured. Crusade members blamed the police for throwing grenades, while police accused the organization of housing explosives. Following this incident, several members were murdered under suspicious circumstances, leaving the Crusade for Justice severely shaken and weakened.

The Crusade for Justice, the Alianza, the Brown Berets, the Raza Unida Party, and just about every other organization in the Chicano Movement were targets of FBI Director J. Edgar Hoover's COINTELPRO program, a covert domestic counterintelligence initiative that included political surveillance and infiltration by FBI agents and local and state police. In one instance, an undercover agent named Frank Martínez infiltrated both the MAYO organization in Texas as well as the Brown Berets in Los Angeles, even cochairing the Chicano Moratorium committee. In his different roles, the agent routinely pushed members to pursue more radical action in order to provoke a police response. Constant surveillance, repeated harassment, mass arrests, infiltration, and conspiracy indictments against leaders eventually wore down many organizations.

On the electoral front, support for the Raza Unida Party continued to dwindle and was further eroded when the perennial candidate for Texas governor, Ramsey Muñiz, was arrested for narcotics trafficking in 1976. Police provocateurs, Democratic Party efforts to undermine the RUP, and internal power struggles further weakened third-party hopes. When Mario Compean ran for Texas governor in 1978, he received less than 2% of the total votes cast. In South Texas, RUP leader José Angel Gutiérrez continued to win elective office, including a Zavala County judgeship, but he faced criticism for his authoritarian leadership and eventually succumbed to Anglo and Mexican American mobilization against him. In 1981, he resigned his post to pursue a career in academia.

Student activism also declined in the latter 1970s as the spirit of militancy gave way to one of individualism. More students chose majors in engineering, business, and professional degrees. Instead of seeing Chicano Studies as a unique discipline fought for by students and scholar activists who demanded that Chicano education reflect its history and community values, the new wave of students saw it as a second-rate major that offered fewer career possibilities. More and more students rejected the term "Chicano," opting for "Hispanic." (Today, "Latino" has become the identifier of choice.) Across the board, activism dwindled and, as the country as a whole became more conservative, many of the gains of the Civil Rights Movement were stalled or rolled back. Chicano historian Rodolfo Acuña refers to the 1970s and 1980s as the age of the Chicano brokers, who, like the Mexican-American Generation, saw negotiation or "brokering" with mainstream society and its institutions as the surest way toward advancement.

WE PREFER THE TERM
HISPANIC BECAUSE, UH,
WELL, JUST BECAUSE.

CORPORATE PROFIT REPORT

AGE OF THE BROKERS

So does all this mean that the Chicano Movement failed? Well, part of the problem is our conventional approach to history, which is to focus on the high-profile events and figures rather than all the moving parts. Although César Chávez, Corky Gonzalez, Reies López Tijerina, and José Angel Gutiérrez—who have been referred to as the Four Horseman of the Chicano Movement—were important to their respective organizations and served as inspirations to many Chicanos, they alone did not create the Movimiento. Rather, it was the thousands of Chicano activists around the country who organized, networked, protested, dialogued, and created an oppositional culture that made the Movimiento what it was. Although many activists gave up protesting altogether, probably more of them just softened their militant approach. The Movement didn't end from one day to the next, or even in a span of years. Instead, the numerous individuals who continued advocating for Mexican American civil rights—whether in education, public policy, electoral politics, or the arts—also continued the spirit of the Chicano Movement.

I began this book by saying that I grew up in a Chicano home in the 1980s and 1990s where the ideology of the Chicano Movement was still very much alive. I'll admit to a certain level of parental indoctrination, but I also understand that the community of activists that surrounded me were part of that larger legacy of the Chicano Movement and that their struggles to improve conditions in Chicano barrios, their protests against U.S. military involvement in Central America and later the Middle East, and their fervent belief that cultural awareness and pride was central to one's being were all threads

leading back to the Chicano Movement, threads that at no point had been severed.

There is now a national holiday in César Chávez's honor (March 31, his birthday); he is the subject of a hagiographic film directed by Diego Luna (*César Chávez,* 2014); and routinely there are calls for his actual sainthood. But none of these accolades captures the fact that, at the time of his death in 1993, three decades after the start of the farmworkers union, Chávez's influence remained as strong as ever with those who continued to advocate on behalf of the working poor. It's true that César Chávez the labor leader had been diminished, his union a shadow of what it once was, but that didn't mean he had failed. From the beginning, Chávez was an inspiration to other Mexican Americans, an example of self-sacrifice, of nonviolent determination, and of perseverance against insurmountable odds. That legacy lived on.

I still remember when my father received the call in 1993 that César Chávez had died. He later told me that his first thought was, "What do we do now?" The "we" implied the Chicano activists that had continued La Causa for so many years.

## DEMOGRAPHICS

The Chicano Movement remains important to this day because many of the issues it addressed remain the same. The K–12 educational system continues to fail Mexican American students; Mexican American students still struggle to gain access to higher education; xenophobia and anti-immigrant hysteria remain fixtures in our political landscape; and the two-party system routinely pays lip service to Mexican American issues without taking meaningful action. One of the key legacies of the Chicano Movement was that it brought the country's attention to the presence of the Mexican American

MY DAD LEARNING THAT CÉSAR HAD DIED.

population. Although Mexican Americans organized and advocated for their civil rights long before the 1960s, they did so mainly in the shadows. The Chicano Movement changed that. Today, it would be hard to ignore or not be aware of the presence of Mexican Americans, not just in the Southwest, but all across the country. But the challenges mentioned above have only been compounded by the fact that the Mexican American population has grown exponentially in recent decades.

According to the Pew Hispanic Research Center, the U.S. Hispanic population increased more than six-fold from 1970 (9.1 million) to the beginning of 2015 (55.4 million). Of those, Mexicans represented the largest national origin group. In California, Latinos became the largest single ethnic group in 2014, representing 39% of the state's population. The last time that was the case was just after Mexico

ceded California to the United States in the 1848 Treaty of Guadalupe Hidalgo. Latinos also make up the majority of California's public school system. The demographic shift has radically altered the political, economic, and educational landscape.

## POLITICS

Although the Raza Unida Party's challenge to the two-party system failed, its efforts helped set precedent and lay the groundwork for further Mexican American participation in electoral politics. In San Antonio, Texas, for example, the twin brothers Julián and Joaquín Castro have risen to political prominence in the 2010s: Julián was elected mayor of San Antonio and Joaquín to the U.S. House of Representatives. Both brothers credit the influence of their mother, Rosie Castro, who served as chairwoman of Bexar County's Raza Unida Party in the early 1970s.

Yet most Latino candidates are careful to disavow radical politics despite what impact they may have had on their political development. In 2005, Antonio Villaraigosa was elected as the first Mexican American mayor of Los Angeles since 1872. Although he had been among the student protestors during the 1968 blowouts and was a member of MEChA while a student at UCLA, he distanced himself from his early activism and was careful to not run as a "Latino" candidate.

While some Mexican American politicians have found their way into local and state office, and to a certain extent onto the national stage, most members of the community face the same dilemma they did a half-century ago. How do Mexican Americans get Democrat or Republican politicians, Latino or otherwise, to pay more than just lip service to the Mexican American community? Because of changing national demographics, the two-party system must pay greater attention to Latino voters—that was even clear to John F. Kennedy in 1960, when his campaign organized the Viva Kennedy! Clubs—but Mexican Americans today continue to fight for their voices to be heard beyond the campaign trail.

## EDUCATION

In 1968, Chicano students walked out of their classrooms demanding changes in the educational system. Challenges still exist today. Although high school dropout rates have fallen, many Mexican American students still attend poorly funded, de facto segregated schools. As a consequence, they face great obstacles in pursuing higher education. Mexican Americans lag far behind their Anglo peers in obtaining bachelor's degrees.

As Mexican Americans form a growing percentage of the national K–12 student population, ensuring their success is essential to the economic well-being of the country. How this is best achieved is a matter of debate, but programs that emerged out of the Civil Rights Movement to help Mexican American and other minority students achieve educational success—such as bilingual education, affirmative action programs, and ethnic studies curricula—are routinely challenged if not scrapped altogether.

In 1996, California voters passed Proposition 209, ending affirmative action. Two years later, they passed Proposition 227, which ended bilingual education in state public schools. More recently, legislators in Arizona passed a bill banning ethnic studies in the high school curriculum. Many Latino-authored books were banned or removed, including two classic Chicano novels—Rudolfo Anaya's *Bless Me, Última* (1972) and Sandra Cisneros's *The House on Mango Street* (1984). Despite studies showing that Mexican American studies courses improve student grades, graduation rates, and college enrollment, opponents have charged that the courses teach hatred.

More than 40 years after student demonstrators demanded a curriculum that included Mexican American contributions to United States history and culture, students and educators were again forced to fight for its survival.

Similarly, while Chicano scholarship has found its footing in academia, the number of Mexican American faculty remains low. From their inception, Chicano Studies departments and programs, as interdisciplinary projects that ran counter to institutional practices, faced uphill battles. They continue to do so today. Many departments and programs still exist, but just as many have been incorporated into American Studies, Latin American Studies, Ethnic Studies, or increasingly, Latino Studies. While these disciplines also focus on issues of race, class, sexuality, and transnationalism, the architects of Chicano Studies saw Mexican American contributions as significant enough to merit its exclusive study. Not only that, they also saw Chicano Studies as a bridge between academia and the Mexican American community. Although this has not disappeared completely, most tenure-track scholars are aware that academic institutions rarely recognize grassroots activism and other nontraditional forms of scholarship. Lastly, in an era where semi-privatized universities are increasingly driven by the bottom line, Chicano Studies remains in a position where it must continually battle for funding. As the population of Mexican Americans increases nationwide, inarguably changing the face of the country, it's clear that the subject deserves not less, but more resources and serious scholarly attention.

## IMMIGRATION

Immigration continues to be a critical and highly sensitive issue facing the United States. But while it is routinely debated on the campaign trail, meaningful changes in policy have been slow in coming. Anti-immigrant hysteria is always around the corner. In 1994,

California governor Pete Wilson helped pushed through Proposition 187, which would have instituted citizenship screening and prohibited undocumented immigrants from using health care or public education. Eventually deemed unconstitutional, similar ballot initiatives and laws continue to be passed across the country, including Arizona Senate Bill 1070, which in 2010 made the failure to carry

WE ARE ALL DREAMERS!

immigration documents a crime and gave police the power to detain anyone they suspected of being in the country illegally. In the post-9/11 era, federal immigration policy has increasingly militarized the border. And though Democrats traditionally have been considered more immigration friendly, President Barack Obama presided over more deportations than any other administration in U.S. history.

Despite the backlash, the immigrant community and its supporters haven't sat idly by. In 2006, mass demonstration throughout the country protested U.S. immigration policy. Millions of people, many of them undocumented immigrants, marched in the streets. In Los Angeles alone, one million demonstrators gathered, including thousands of students who walked out of their classrooms in support of immigrants. Many cited the influence of the 1968 Chicano blowouts, and it was hard not to view the mass demonstrations as part of a long continuum of civil rights struggles demanding that the United States live up to its ideals of equality and justice for all.

In 2012, President Obama initiated the Deferred Action for Childhood Arrivals (DACA), which gave undocumented immigrants brought to the country as children a path to permanent residency. Obama acted upon strong pressure from the self-described "Dreamers," young undocumented immigrants who often placed themselves at risk in order to have their voices heard. Their activism was again reminiscent of the courageous young people of the 1960s who rose up and demanded change from the powers that be. In June 2016, however, a deadlocked U.S. Supreme Court let stand a lower-court ruling that effectively blocked the Obama initiative.

## IDENTITY AND CULTURAL PRIDE

The Chicano Movement and the cultural renaissance it spawned continue to be felt to the present day. Although Mexican American visual artists, authors, playwrights, musicians, actors, and filmmakers struggle to find a mainstream audience, the breadth of artistic work still being created reveals the complexity of the Mexican American experience. Although not all Mexican American artists consider themselves Chicano, or see their work as part of the Chicano tradition, the fact is that Chicano artists in the 1960s and 1970s were the first to tackle head on issues related to their bicultural identity and their marginalization in American society. They were the first to create whole, fully developed Latino characters that countered the stereotypes found in Hollywood films and popular media. This important precedent allowed subsequent artists to take their work in completely new directions.

As a writer and artist myself, I understand the privilege of being able to stand before a blank page and express myself knowing that my cultural experience is as valid as anyone's and that I draw upon a rich, multifaceted history. Before the Chicano Movement, Mexican Americans were made to feel ashamed of who they were. Their language, culture, and history were denigrated, and the only possibility of escaping a lifetime of indignity was to shed these markers of difference. Being proud of who you are doesn't seem like a radical statement, but for Mexican Americans it is one of the Chicano Movement's most important legacies.

# FURTHER READING

Acuña, Rodolfo. *Occupied America: A History of Chicanos.* 8th ed. Boston: Pearson, 2015.

Anzaldúa, Gloria. *Borderlands/La Frontera: The New Mestiza.* 4th ed. San Francisco: Aunt Lute Books, 2012.

Blackwell, Maylei. *¡Chicana Power!: Contested Histories of Feminism in the Chicano Movement.* Austin: University of Texas Press, 2011.

Busto, Rudy V. *King Tiger: The Religious Vision of Reies López Tijerina.* Albuquerque: University of New Mexico Press, 2005.

García, Ignacio M. *United We Win: The Rise and Fall of La Raza Unida Party.* Tucson: University of Arizona Press, 1989.

García, Mario T., and Sal Castro. *Blowout! Sal Castro & the Chicano Struggle for Educational Justice.* Chapel Hill: University of North Carolina Press, 2011.

Gómez-Quiñones, Juan, and Irene Vásquez. *Making Aztlán: Ideology and Culture of the Chicana and Chicano Movement, 1966–1977.* Albuquerque: University of New Mexico Press, 2014.

Ferriss, Susan, and Ricardo Sandoval. *The Fight in the Fields: Cesar Chavez and the Farm Workers Union.* New York: Harcourt Brace, 1997.

Jackson, Carlos F. *Chicana and Chicano Art: ProtestArte (The Mexican American Experience).* Tucson: University of Arizona Press, 2009.

Levy, Jacques E. *Cesar Chavez: Autobiography of La Causa.* Minneapolis: University of Minnesota, 2007.

López, Tiffany A. *Growing up Chicana/o: An Anthology.* New York: William Morrow, 1995.

Mariscal, George. *Aztlán and Viet Nam: Chicano and Chicana Experiences of the War.* Berkeley: University of California Press, 1999.

Mariscal, George. *Brown-Eyed Children of the Sun: Lessons from the Chicano Movement, 1965–1975.* Albuquerque: University of New Mexico Press, 2005.

Martínez, Elizabeth. *500 Years of Chicana Women's History.* New Brunswick, NJ: Rutgers University Press, 2008.

Muñoz, Carlos. *Youth, Identity, Power: The Chicano Movement.* London and New York: Verso, 1989.

Oropeza, Lorena. *¡Raza Sí! ¡Guerra No!: Chicano Protest and Patriotism During the Viet Nam War Era.* Berkeley: University of California Press, 2005.

Rebolledo, Tey D., and Eliana S. Rivero, eds. *Infinite Divisions: An Anthology of Chicana Literature.* Tucson: University of Arizona Press, 1993.

Rosales, Francisco Arturo. *Chicano! The History of the Mexican American Civil Rights Movement.* Houston: Arte Público Press, 1996.

Ruiz, Vicki L. *From Out of the Shadows: Mexican Women in Twentieth-Century America.* 10th ed. New York: Oxford University Press, 2008.

Vigil, Ernesto B. *The Crusade for Justice: Chicano Militancy and the Government's War on Dissent.* Madison: University of Wisconsin Press, 1999.

# ABOUT THE AUTHOR AND ILLUSTRATOR

Writer, artist, and educator MACEO MONTOYA is an assistant professor in the Department of Chicano Studies at the University of California, Davis, where he teaches courses in Chicano Literature and the Chicana/o Mural Workshop. He is also the director of Taller Arte del Nuevo Amenecer (TANA), a community-based art center in Woodland, California. Professor Montoya is the author of several acclaimed works of fiction, including *The Scoundrel and the Optimist* (2010), *The Deportation of Wopper Barraza: A Novel* (2014), and *You Must Fight Them: A Novella and Stories* (2015). *Letters to the Poet from His Brother* (2014) is a hybrid work combining images, prose poems, and essays. His paintings, drawings, and prints have been widely exhibited and published. Learn more about him and his work at *www.maceomontoya.com*.

# THE FOR BEGINNERS® SERIES

ABSTRACT EXPRESSIONISM     ISBN 978-1-939994-62-2
AFRICAN HISTORY FOR BEGINNERS     ISBN 978-1-934389-18-8
ANARCHISM FOR BEGINNERS     ISBN 978-1-934389-32-4
ARABS & ISRAEL FOR BEGINNERS     ISBN 978-1-934389-16-4
ART THEORY FOR BEGINNERS     ISBN 978-1-934389-47-8
ASTRONOMY FOR BEGINNERS     ISBN 978-1-934389-25-6
AYN RAND FOR BEGINNERS     ISBN 978-1-934389-37-9
BARACK OBAMA FOR BEGINNERS, AN ESSENTIAL GUIDE     ISBN 978-1-934389-44-7
BEN FRANKLIN FOR BEGINNERS     ISBN 978-1-934389-48-5
BLACK HISTORY FOR BEGINNERS     ISBN 978-1-934389-19-5
THE BLACK HOLOCAUST FOR BEGINNERS     ISBN 978-1-934389-03-4
BLACK PANTHERS FOR BEGINNERS     ISBN 978-1-939994-39-4
BLACK WOMEN FOR BEGINNERS     ISBN 978-1-934389-20-1
BUDDHA FOR BEGINNERS     ISBN 978-1-939994-33-2
BUKOWSKI FOR BEGINNERS     ISBN 978-1-939994-37-0
CHOMSKY FOR BEGINNERS     ISBN 978-1-934389-17-1
CIVIL RIGHTS FOR BEGINNERS     ISBN 978-1-934389-89-8
CLIMATE CHANGE FOR BEGINNERS     ISBN 978-1-939994-43-1
DADA & SURREALISM FOR BEGINNERS     ISBN 978-1-934389-00-3
DANTE FOR BEGINNERS     ISBN 978-1-934389-67-6
DECONSTRUCTION FOR BEGINNERS     ISBN 978-1-934389-26-3
DEMOCRACY FOR BEGINNERS     ISBN 978-1-934389-36-2
DERRIDA FOR BEGINNERS     ISBN 978-1-934389-11-9
EASTERN PHILOSOPHY FOR BEGINNERS     ISBN 978-1-934389-07-2
EXISTENTIALISM FOR BEGINNERS     ISBN 978-1-934389-21-8
FANON FOR BEGINNERS     ISBN 978-1-934389-87-4
FDR AND THE NEW DEAL FOR BEGINNERS     ISBN 978-1-934389-50-8
FOUCAULT FOR BEGINNERS     ISBN 978-1-934389-12-6
FRENCH REVOLUTIONS FOR BEGINNERS     ISBN 978-1-934389-91-1
GENDER & SEXUALITY FOR BEGINNERS     ISBN 978-1-934389-69-0
GREEK MYTHOLOGY FOR BEGINNERS     ISBN 978-1-934389-83-6
HEIDEGGER FOR BEGINNERS     ISBN 978-1-934389-13-3
THE HISTORY OF CLASSICAL MUSIC FOR BEGINNERS     ISBN 978-1-939994-26-4
THE HISTORY OF OPERA FOR BEGINNERS     ISBN 978-1-934389-79-9
ISLAM FOR BEGINNERS     ISBN 978-1-934389-01-0
JANE AUSTEN FOR BEGINNERS     ISBN 978-1-934389-61-4
JUNG FOR BEGINNERS     ISBN 978-1-934389-76-8
KIERKEGAARD FOR BEGINNERS     ISBN 978-1-934389-14-0
LACAN FOR BEGINNERS     ISBN 978-1-934389-39-3
LIBERTARIANISM FOR BEGINNERS     ISBN 978-1-939994-66-0
LINCOLN FOR BEGINNERS     ISBN 978-1-934389-85-0
LINGUISTICS FOR BEGINNERS     ISBN 978-1-934389-28-7
MALCOLM X FOR BEGINNERS     ISBN 978-1-934389-04-1
MARX'S DAS KAPITAL FOR BEGINNERS     ISBN 978-1-934389-59-1
MCLUHAN FOR BEGINNERS     ISBN 978-1-934389-75-1
MORMONISM FOR BEGINNERS     ISBN 978-1-939994-52-3
MUSIC THEORY FOR BEGINNERS     ISBN 978-1-939994-46-2
NIETZSCHE FOR BEGINNERS     ISBN 978-1-934389-05-8
PAUL ROBESON FOR BEGINNERS     ISBN 978-1-934389-81-2
PHILOSOPHY FOR BEGINNERS     ISBN 978-1-934389-02-7
PLATO FOR BEGINNERS     ISBN 978-1-934389-08-9
POETRY FOR BEGINNERS     ISBN 978-1-934389-46-1
POSTMODERNISM FOR BEGINNERS     ISBN 978-1-934389-09-6
PROUST FOR BEGINNERS     ISBN 978-1-939994-44-8
RELATIVITY & QUANTUM PHYSICS FOR BEGINNERS     ISBN 978-1-934389-42-3
SARTRE FOR BEGINNERS     ISBN 978-1-934389-15-7
SAUSSURE FOR BEGINNERS     ISBN 978-1-939994-41-7
SHAKESPEARE FOR BEGINNERS     ISBN 978-1-934389-29-4
STANISLAVSKI FOR BEGINNERS     ISBN 978-1-939994-35-6
STRUCTURALISM & POSTSTRUCTURALISM FOR BEGINNERS     ISBN 978-1-934389-10-2
WOMEN'S HISTORY FOR BEGINNERS     ISBN 978-1-934389-60-7
UNIONS FOR BEGINNERS     ISBN 978-1-934389-77-5
U.S. CONSTITUTION FOR BEGINNERS     ISBN 978-1-934389-62-1
ZEN FOR BEGINNERS     ISBN 978-1-934389-06-5
ZINN FOR BEGINNERS     ISBN 978-1-934389-40-9